DATE DUE

Feb 1869.			
Mar 12 '69			
Mar 8 '71			
Apr 20 '71			
May 3 '71			
Sep 28 '71			
Oct 11 '71			
Oct 25 '71			
Oct 12 '72			
Mar 13 '73			
Mar 27 '73			
Nov 26 '74			
GAYLORD			PRINTED IN U.S.A.

GEORGE WASHINGTON CARVER:
The Man Who Overcame

GEORGE WASHINGTON CARVER:

The Man Who Overcame

by
Lawrence Elliott

Prentice-Hall, Inc. Englewood Cliffs, N. J.

George Washington Carver: The Man Who Overcame
by Lawrence Elliott

© 1966 by Lawrence Elliott
All rights reserved. No part of this book may be reproduced in any
form or by any means, except for the inclusion of brief quotations
in a review, without permission in writing from the publisher.
Library of Congress Catalog Card Number: 66-23368
Printed in the United States of America
T 35390

PRENTICE-HALL INTERNATIONAL, INC., *London*
PRENTICE-HALL OF AUSTRALIA, PTY. LTD., *Sydney*
PRENTICE-HALL OF CANADA, LTD., *Toronto*
PRENTICE-HALL OF INDIA PRIVATE LTD., *New Delhi*
PRENTICE-HALL OF JAPAN, INC., *Tokyo*

A PEGASUS BOOK
from
THE READER'S DIGEST PRESS

For JAIN, BETTY and BARBARA
Whose world will shut no
doors on its George Carvers

Acknowledgments

In a very real sense, this biography is the collected recollections of the great number of people who have good reason to remember Dr. Carver. I am deeply grateful to all of them.

My special thanks go to Dr. Luther H. Foster, president of Tuskegee Institute, who caused all doors to be opened to me during my research stay there in the spring of 1964; and to Mrs. W. Edward Belton, who led me through them. Members of the Tuskegee Institute faculty and community were unfailingly generous with their time and reminiscences. I particularly want to thank Dr. Clarence T. Mason, director of the Carver Foundation at Tuskegee; Mrs. Juanita Jones; L. A. Locklair; Dr. Reuben A. Munday; Edward W. Ramsey; George Scott; Harry Waggener; Harold Webb; and John Welch.

Others who knew Dr. Carver at Tuskegee and who contributed significantly to this work are William L. Dawson, a music teacher in the Carver era; Harry O. Abbott, the aging professor's ever-resourceful travelling companion; and, of course, Austin W. Curtis, Carver's beloved assistant, who was able to provide me with so much pertinent material available nowhere else.

At the George Washington Carver National Monument in Diamond, Missouri, Historian Robert P. Fuller shared with me the fruits of his careful research of the Moses Carver family and George Carver's early years. Dr. Frederick D. Patterson, president of Tuskegee Institute during Carver's last years and now president of the Phelps-Stokes Foundation, graciously talked of his memories and feelings for the great scientist. Dr. John W. Chenault recalled for me the period when he assisted Dr. Carver in the treatment of those hundreds of polio victims who found their way to the laboratory on the Tuskegee campus. Miss Ruth Jackson, of the English Department at Simpson College in Iowa, wrote me at length about Carver's student days there and his association with the Milhollands and Etta Budd. I want to thank them all.

Former President Harry S. Truman, Secretary of Agriculture Orville L. Freeman, and the late Henry A. Wallace were most generous in their replies to my questions, and I am genuinely grateful to each of them.

Finally, and in the truest tradition, I must thank my wife, who typed this manuscript, caught my errors, weighed my ideas and bore my complaints, and in ways large and small sustained me through this writing.

Lawrence Elliott
Babylon, N.Y.
March 28, 1966

Foreword

THE RARE PRIVILEGE of working closely with Dr. Carver during the last fourteen years of his life gave me an unusual opportunity to observe the several facets of this extremely unusual man. His humility of spirit and simplicity of manner were as disarming as his keen intellect and wide ranging knowledge were a source of inspiration and challenge. These impressions were of a Dr. Carver, fully mature and renowned because of his discoveries and a life-long dedication of service to his fellowman through the practical applications of science. At this stage his life had become an almost perfect blend of the spiritual, the artistic, and the scientific.

The Man Who Overcame by Lawrence Elliott tells better than any book I have read how Dr. Carver got to be the man he was in the closing years of his maturity.

This volume is delightfully and entertainingly written. It reveals Carver's genius as a flickering spark almost snubbed out in the body of a sickly infant and traces its growth to fullest brilliance through the great variety of experiences which were in turn rewarding and repressing but never quite totally subduing to his indomitable spirit.

This biography, like those of many great men, reveals with adequate illustrative support that Carver's eminence resulted from the combination of his innate gifts, years of continuous and increasing study, and unceasing application to a variety of tasks which consumed every conscious moment.

Carver's dedication to the basic needs of his fellowman without regard to race led to an increasing exploration of all available natural resources. The successful fashioning of these to improve the life of the region identified Tuskegee Institute with the local and national community and gave it a reputation for excellence which could not have been attained from classroom instruction. The author reveals the extent to which Booker T. Washington and George Washington Carver, though highly diverse in personality and talent, found a common meeting ground in their dedication to the erasure of human want. Thus Carver's work became in the fullest sense the practical implementation of Booker Washington's philosophy. Elliott's book on Carver is a contribution of significant value to those who would understand the capacity of human beings to transcend barriers of race in accomplishment and human service. More than this, the Carver story redefines the true meaning of education.

Frederick D. Patterson

Contents

GEORGE WASHINGTON CARVER:

The Man Who Overcame

I. The Slave Who
Freed the South

MEASURE ME NOT BY THE HEIGHTS TO
WHICH I HAVE CLIMBED BUT THE DEPTHS
FROM WHICH I HAVE COME.

—*Frederick Douglass*

SOME SAY he was the most remarkable American who ever lived. No one knew more about the chemical magic locked in a plant, nor how better to turn it to man's use. Working in a laboratory equipped with the salvage of the garbage dump, using rusted pans and improvised beakers, he separated the mysterious particles of matter and fused them into new foods and medicines and building materials.

He ground colors from native clays and, with his fingers, painted pictures so beautiful that galleries and museums begged to buy them. No, he said, then gave them away to his friends, and today they hang in humble homes in Detroit and Chicago and Tuskegee, Alabama. He made pie from peanuts and salads from weeds, and the great hotels used his recipes. With no formal training he became a concert pianist and toured the country to raise money for the obscure little college where he taught. A few years later, without serious second thought, he turned down an invitation to work for Edison

1

at a salary of $100,000 a year. He kept saying that he had no time to marry, but if you wrote asking for some flower seeds he found time to send them to you, and if he passed your front door and your roses looked wan, he would stop and tell you what ailed them.

Presidents Coolidge and Franklin Roosevelt came to see him. Foreign governments sought his counsel, as did plain people everywhere, and Henry Wallace and Ford and Gandhi were his friends.

And all the while countless doors were closed in his face.

No human ever had a less auspicious start in life. He never knew his mother or father, nor even the year he first saw the light of day. He was a Negro, born a slave early in the bloody civil war that ended legal slavery. He came into the world sickly and was made worse, and it seemed certain that he would die in his swaddling clothes. And having survived by some freakish suspension of the laws of nature, he ought to have grown up twisted and bitter and maimed in spirit, for day by day it was hammered into his people that they were little better than field oxen, and they were sometimes treated worse. But all his long life he refuted that lie. Nor could he harbor malice against those who spoke it: though the world he looked out on was not always sunny, it remained forever hopeful.

He was well past thirty when his schooling years were done with. From town to town in the frontier Midwest he had hungered after knowledge, trading his labor for lessons wherever he could find a school willing to admit a black boy. The open road was much his home in all the years of his youth, and hunger and cold his most steadfast companions. But he kept moving and trying and learning, and at last the spark of his soaring creativity flamed up, and it burned ever after with a brilliant glow.

His discoveries freed the South from the tyranny of King Cotton. He restored the essence of life to millions of spent and sterile acres, then found a vigorous new crop with which to sow them. Those who could never bring themselves to break bread with him, or even to call him "Mister," prospered by his genius, and blessed it. He brightened the homes of impoverished men and women throughout the old Confederacy, and he gave to their children a measure of hope. And someday it will be seen that, without ever addressing himself to the indignities heaped on black men in a white world, he did more than any single soul to bring on the day when both will live peaceably, equally, side by side.

His name was George W. Carver, and every day that he lived he labored toward some tangible end that would make this earth a little richer, or healthier, or lovelier, for all men—black, white, yellow and red. And when he died all those who lived, and had yet to live, were suddenly poorer.

II. The Ransom was a Racehorse

> I T-TOOK AND REPLANTED THE ROSES,
> MA'AM. IN THE S-S-SUN. ROSES WANT
> S-S-SUN, MA'AM.
>
> —*Carver's George*

It was the worst of times. All the land was racked by the war between North and South, and to the farmers and plainsmen of Missouri the sum of the nation's agony seemed pent within the borders of their state. Most owned a slave or two to help them plow that stubborn sod, true enough, but they had voted to stay with Abe Lincoln and the Union. And now their plains were a no-man's-land, their farms a battleground. Jayhawkers from free Kansas and bushwhackers from secessionist Arkansas bloodied the countryside as they clashed and clashed again. Guerillas and plain bandits rode the land, pillaging and killing. They came by night to burn fields and homes and barns, it didn't matter whose; to steal live-stock and spirit slaves south to Louisana and Texas where they could be put on the block for swollen wartime prices.

On the Ozark plateau, near the settlement of Diamond Grove, Moses Carver felt the terrorist lash. Masked men galloped into his farmyard on a winter's night and, wiring his thumbs, strung him up on a walnut tree. They whipped him and burned his bare feet with coals from the fire while Susan, his wife, writhed in their grasp and moaned in helplessness, anguish. And all the time they bawled, "Where's your money hid? Where's your niggers, you Yankee hypocrite?"

His body cried out for succor, but no sound passed Moses Carver's lips. He had labored long and hard for the little he owned, and there was iron at the core of his being: he would die before he gave in to these bushwhackers. And presently the masked men mistook the nervous stomping of Carver's horses for the approach of a posse and, firing an empty barn in vengefulness and panic, they rode into the dark.

Susan cut her man down from the walnut tree. She put plantain leaves on his seared feet, weeping quietly. Neither of them spoke until, at last, Moses told her to go and fetch out Mary, the slave girl, and Mary's babies, from the hiding place in the cave below the milkhouse. Then he sat alone in the log house, breathing heavily, the flames from his burning barn glaring and dancing in the cabin's single window, and he thought what utter madness it was. He had worked so hard. He had fought gales and drought and the bitter loneliness of the frontier. And now to have these men—human beings, like himself— intent on undoing the toil of nearly all his adult years was almost more than he could grasp.

For Moses Carver knew in his bones that this was not the last of it. The nightriders would be back.

He was well into his middle years, a lean, bearded man whose strength showed plainly in a stiff, seamed face. He could trace his ancestry back nearly 150 years, back to the time when his people, seeking freedom and elbow room, had left England for the New World. Generation by generation they pushed west into virgin country. Moses had been born on the Ohio frontier in 1812 and, at twenty, he, too, was moving on. In Illinois he took himself a wife, Miss Susan Blue, and together they came down the river into Missouri country, crossing the plain and coming, at last, to the walnut groves and green meadows at the foot of the Ozarks. And here they filed a claim on a 160-acre homestead, hard by the Arkansas line.

It was an unrelenting life. A bitter winter wind swept down from the mountains, and in summer there seemed no escape from the malevolent heat. They lost their one baby, a girl, only days after she was born, and God had not seen fit to bless them with another.

But Moses Carver was an unrelenting man. He fought the sod and the wind and the sun. He built a sound cabin, and with Susan's help he cleared the land, and where there had been wilderness there was now a proper farm. He raised horses, good horses, and others who came to settle the country said that Moses Carver was the fairest, hardest-working man in all Newton County.

He had odd ideas though. For one thing, he didn't hold with church-going—yet he had given a parcel of his land to be used as a burying place for the people of Diamond Grove, and stood in solemn silence while the preacher consecrated it. For another, he spoke out bitterly against slavery—it was sinful, he said, immoral. And yet he had bought himself a slave girl.

No one, not even Susan, knew the torment in Moses' soul at passing money over the body of another human. He owned no field hand as the other farmers did. With his bare hands—and such rare hired help as might now and then come wandering through—he had done every menial and backbreaking job that needed doing on a frontier farm. And so it would always be, he vowed. But the loneliness and the long years had begun to tell on his wife. Susan had begged him to get her a girl, someone to help with the yard chores, someone to talk to during the endless hours when he was in the fields. And so six years before, Moses had gone to his neighbor, Colonel James Grant, and paid $700 for Mary. She was thirteen years old then, a good girl, bright and gentle and singing at her work, and soon it was as though she had always been one of the family. When she had her young ones, they, too, became part of the Carver household, those that lived— two infant girls lay buried at the foot of the hill, where Susan's own baby had been laid to rest. But treating Mary decently had not wholly lulled Moses' conscience. Slavery was slavery, and trafficking in one human was no different from trafficking in a hundred.

And now, on this piercing cold winter night, Moses Carver found himself doubly torn. The raiders would be back, of that he was certain. If they found the money he had hidden under the beehive, that was one thing. But if they stole his Mary and sold her into bondage in some faraway place, then he would carry that guilt all the rest of his days.

Carver's Mary couldn't even trace her ancestry back to her mother. She had sprung to life, like so many of her people, seemingly without human help or love. Now she sat in the one-room shanty where she lived with her babies and pressed the newborn boy to her breast. Almost without pause his frail body shook and heaved with a racking cough, and Mary felt that if she did not hold him very tightly, praying life from her body to his, he would surely die.

Swaying in her chair, she crooned a fragment of melody, her soft dark eyes on little Jim and four-year-old Melissa. They lay stiffly awake in the trundle bed, held yet by the fear of that cowering time in the dark cave.

"Close your eyes. Go to sleep now," Mary told them.

But still they stared tautly into the firelight, and still their mother rocked to and fro, the choking baby pressed close to her flesh. She felt old and weary and knowing, far beyond her years. She had come to believe that her people were forever marked for affliction and she was afraid that her own sorrows were not done with yet. She had buried two babies and the one she now held seemed to be spewing up his very life in her arms. She had had a good man and with the first snow—the new baby wasn't two months old—they had sent over from the Grant plantation to tell her that he was dead.

"He was hauling logs," they said, eyes on the ground, "and the ox bolted. Giles fell off. A log rolled over him . . ."

There was more—they talked for a long time—but Carver's Mary hadn't heard. Giles was dead and the rest didn't matter. She thought about him for a while, how he used to come over from the Grant place when he could and sit with her on the shanty doorstep, and the night was never so dark when he was there. She thought about her little-girl days on the big plantation, about the great brick house and the shanties out behind where the slaves sat on the ground of a summer evening and sang the sad songs of their hopeless hope. Their yearning and their ingrained grief was beyond her then. In a child's way she felt sorry for them because they wouldn't be happy. But now she understood. For all the Carvers' kindness, she was one with her people, and their curse was on her, too.

The baby coughed and writhed as the breath strangled in his throat. She put a spoonful of honey and tansy to his lips and he gagged, then breathed raggedly again.

No, there would be no end to her sorrow. The masked men would come back and, sooner or later, they would take her away.

They came in the week before Christmas, on a night when the wind shrieked and slashed at the land. As in a dream Moses heard the pounding of their horses' hoofs on the frozen road from Diamond Grove and he sprang from his bed. "Run to the cave!" he ordered Susan. And hobbling on blistered feet toward the shanty, stumbling through the black night, he cried out, "Wake up, Mary! They're coming!"

He flung open her door and the horsemen had not yet turned into the farm, and he thought wildly: there's time; there's still time! But Mary stood motionless by the dying fire, her eyes fixed on some faraway place, as though she hadn't heard and didn't understand. She held the sick baby to her. The child Melissa clung to her nightdress.

"In the name of heaven, girl, move!" Moses called. "They'll be on us in another minute!"

She seemed to stir, to look around her for one last thing before fleeing. Moses snatched the sleeping Jim up from the trundle bed and tried to take the little girl's hand. But she had been frightened by the tumult and tried to bury her face against her mother's leg.

"Bring the girl," Moses said, starting for the door. "And stay right behind me!"

The blistering wind tore into the open cabin. Desperately Mary's eyes searched the tiny room—she must have warm clothing for her sick child, a blanket!—and all the while the gathering clatter of the horses grew louder in her ears. She ran to one corner, then another, blindly, uselessly, until finally the masked men had bounded into the shanty and wrenched the babies from her arms, flinging her back against the log wall. They tied her wrists behind her. They shoved her up on a horse and threw a shawl over her shoulders. Stunned by the abrupt cold, trembling, she begged, "Please cover my babies."

There was no reply, only the harsh breathing of men in a rush to be mounted and gone, and in another moment the horses were pelting down the dark road.

"They've got her," Moses whispered to his wife when he heard that sound. "They wouldn't be gone so quickly if they hadn't found what they came for."

"Mary, Mary," Susan Carver wept into the blackness of the cave, clutching Mary's little Jim in her arms.

And Moses closed his eyes and said, "Lord forgive me."

In the morning, trailing a racehorse, he rode into Diamond Grove and sought out a man named Bentley. For it had come to Moses Carver near the end of that sleepless night that there was yet a chance to get Mary back. John Bentley had once ridden with the bushwhackers, people said, though he now proclaimed himself a Unionist, and it might just be that one of their own would know where to catch up with the nightriders. Now, standing in a biting wind on the wood sidewalk outside the general store, Moses Carver wasted no words:

"They stole my Mary and two of her young ones last night, Bentley. I'm not asking into your business, but if you know where they're headed, I'll pay you to go after them. Take Pacer—he's one of my best horses, you can see—and ransom her."

Bentley rubbed his long jaw. "What's in it for me?" he asked.

"Bring the girl back and I'll give you 40 acres of timberland," Moses Carver said.

And so the bargain was made and, before noontime, Bentley was riding south. Then the hours were long for Moses and Susan Carver. Every falling walnut sounded like a horse's hoof on their path, and in the stern winter twilight, sometimes a bush bending to the everlasting wind seemed like a girl hunched in the cold and coming home, at last. When night fell, they sat silent by the fire, two-year-old Jim playing at their feet. There was nothing to say, nor anything to do, only wait.

They waited five days. Christmas came and went, a bleak, cheerless time. Moses began to envision Bentley in some Arkansas saloon, wiping whiskey off that long jaw and laughing as he told how a dim-witted Yankee farmer had given him—given him, mind you!—a $300 racehorse out of some fool notion that he actually meant to go chasing after a bunch of bushwhackers who had his slave girl. Then, on the sixth day, in a cold, driving rain, in the late afternoon, there *was* a sound on their path. Moses ran to throw open the door, Susan trying to crowd past him. And it was Bentley. And he was alone, riding his own horse and trailing the racehorse behind.

They watched, numb and speechless, as he dismounted stiffly and clumped into the house, drippings marking his every step. He took a damp and dirty bundle from under

his coat and held it out to them in his two hands, but neither made a move to touch it. "It's all I got," Bentley said.
"I don't know whether it's alive or dead."

"The baby!" Susan cried, and snatched the filthy parcel to her. "The baby," she whispered, fumbling the rags
open and peering down into the pinched dark face of
Mary's child. The boy's lips and eyelids were tinged with
blue and he lay still in her arms, like a newborn sparrow
who had died in the nest.

She ran to heat milk, then fell to her knees on the
hearth, stripping the wet homespun away from the tiny
body. She held him naked by the fire, as close as she
dared, squeezing his scrawny chest, ordering Moses after
the warm milk and a pinch of sugar to put into it. Holding a spoonful to the blue lips, her face grew tense and
white as the milk trickled uselessly on the infant's chin.
Then he choked, cried feebly, and sucked for more.

"He's alive! At least he's alive," she said, and tears
welled in her eyes.

John Bentley stood staring, dumfounded, unable to
comprehend how anyone could get so wrought up over
a sick nigger brat. Still, when he spoke, his voice was
soft. "I'm sorry about the girl. I never did catch up with
that gang." He jerked a thumb at the wheezing child and
said, "Reckon I couldn't take your timberland for just
that."

Moses tried to tear his eyes from the awesome tableau
by the fireplace—the baby clinging to a bare shred of
life, and his Susan fighting tenaciously, heedlessly, to
strengthen his precarious grip. Carefully she fed droplets
of sweetened milk to the blue lips, waiting patiently
through violent paroxysms of coughing, murmuring,
"Hush now. Hush, little boy."

"Keep the horse," Moses said to Bentley. "You did your best. You brought the boy back."

Bentley nodded. He was satisfied.

"Do you know where they went?" Moses asked.

"South. Deep south. I rode near half across Arkansas and they was still a day ahead of me and riding hard for the Mississippi." He had lost the trail in the high hill country, he said, and finally turned back. He told how he had first heard that Mary was dead, then that she'd been sold to some soldiers headed north. "But I think she was still with them. I think they mean to sell her downriver, her and the other kid, both."

"And this one? The boy?" Moses said unevenly. "Where did you . . . ?"

"Oh, him. They just give him to some womenfolks down by Conway. He ain't worth nothin'."

He was called George, Carver's George, and all his first years were a persistent struggle for survival. Puny and frail, he fell victim to every childhood ill and each one threatened, finally, to drag him through death's door. But in the end, Susan's dogged nursing—and some mysterious, unsuspected toughness in the boy's own meager breast—fought off what seemed surely to be his inevitable dark destiny. The unending cough had torn his vocal cords, so that his voice was like the chirp of a frightened bird. And some traumatic memory, perhaps the same racial fear that haunted Mary, had knotted his tongue and left him with a pitiful stammer. He was nearly three before he could cross the cabin floor unaided, an adventure that set him panting with exhaustion and triumph. But he lived, and that was the greatest triumph of all.

The war ended. The burned barns were rebuilt and

the fields seeded, and soon they showed green to the
spring sun. "You're free now," Moses told George and the
older brother, Jim. "All the slaves are free now. You can
go any place you like."

George didn't understand and Jim just grinned.

"Aunt Susan and me, we'd like you to stay on, same as
before. But bear in mind you're not obliged to. The slaves
are free."

Jim nodded, and that was all that was ever said. That
night the two boys crawled up into the cabin loft and
went to sleep on their ticks stuffed with cornhusks, the
same as they'd always done. It would be a long time before Carver's George found out what Uncle Moses meant,
what it meant to be free. And Jim would never find out.

Jim was soon husky enough to shear sheep and help
with the haying and milking. And Moses, nearing sixty
years, was glad to have the strong brown boy alongside
him in the fields. But George, still fighting for a firm hold
on life, rarely strayed far from the kitchen. He looked
like a bird still, stunted, his dark eyes too big for the
darker face, his arms and legs spindly as reeds. He followed Aunt Susan the day long, aping her movements
as she swept the floor and scraped the tin plates clean.
"Here," she said to him one morning, thrusting the broom
into his hands. "No sense you going through all that mo-
tion for nothing."

He was ecstatic and swept vigorously away, grinning
back at her grin when their eyes met. As the months
passed, he did other chores, laundry and dishwashing
and even cooking, and he did them zestfully, humming
a pensive little tune that sometimes caught at Susan's
heart with its poignant reminder of Mary. Now and then,
when she was in the garden or at the well and George

thought she wouldn't hear, he invented words for his private song, and he sang it in that thin high pitch, but without the trace of a stammer.

There was much to do, for the frontier farm was a world unto itself. To bank on anyone or anything beyond the split rail fence was to court disaster. So George watched Aunt Susan spinning wool or flax for clothing, and soon he was efficiently pumping the treadle. He learned to tan hides and make shoes and cure bacon. There were vegetables to be planted and weeded and canned. There were candles and soap to make, spices to be ground and, when someone took sick, roots to be dug for Aunt Susan to brew into medicine. Nothing was wasted and only sugar and coffee came from the town. And these years of prudence and resourcefulness were to shape the life of Carver's George.

He had a restless curiosity, a zeal to learn, and it never occurred to him that there was anything odd in a boy doing woman's work. It needed doing and with his quick hands and an agile mind, there was little he was loath to try. One spring afternoon, watching Aunt Susan knitting, he suddenly said, "I c-can do that." And using a turkey feather from the yard and an old unraveled mitten, he sat by her side and taught himself to knit. By summer he was crocheting and embroidering. When Aunt Susan started a crazy quilt, she had only to explain the overall pattern to him. Then they started in separate corners, sewing in every odd scrap of fabric that fell into their hands, and when it was done Susan defied Moses to tell the boy's stitches from hers.

Moses had his own reason to be gratefully astonished at George's ingenuity. For weeks his workshoes had tortured him. "I'm just no good as a cobbler," he complained in disgust and, desperate for relief, he even cut the heels from his socks. Still he limped and swore and soaked massive blisters each night. On one such evening, George quietly took both shoes completely apart and remade the heels, then rewove the homespun socks so no one could tell they'd ever been cut, and said, "T-try them now, Uncle Moses." They fit perfectly, and never troubled again.

Often Aunt Susan and George sat on the bench beside the rain barrel, an aging, white-haired woman and a sprite of a black boy, sewing together in the long twilight before Moses and Jim came in from the fields. George would ask where the sun went after it dropped behind the hill, and what made the rain fall, and why the roses by the door were yellow and those under the window red. Sometimes Susan talked about his mother, and then he listened very quietly. "She was quick, like you. She couldn't read, but she remembered, and once we used a recipe in the almanac she could find it again any time."

Once George asked if his mother would ever come back and Susan told him no, it wasn't likely.

Another spring came. George took to slipping off into the woods, to a secret glade he had discovered where nature paraded all her wonders if a person would only look and listen. He poked beneath tree bark and watched the insects crawl. He studied the wildflowers, those that sought the sun and those that managed in shade. He listened to the croak of a frog and the sweet din of the birds, and he felt within him an urgent longing to understand this magically complex world, to know every single thing about it. Why did the night crawlers flee from the sun's warmth? And why couldn't the lilies survive without it?

Why did roots that looked exactly the same produce an astonishing array of different-colored flowers? And what happened to the soft white fluff that came out of the milkweed pod when it opened?

He loved the feel of the warm earth in his hands. Years later, remembering, he would say, "People murder a child when they say, 'keep out of the dirt!' In dirt there is life." On the darkest day he was unafraid in the woods, and was soon more at home in the glade than in the Carver cabin. Hours fled as he sat perched on his knees, watching a fern, marveling at the brave way it poked up through the winter's accumulation of dead leaves. The ferns and flowers and gourds became the toys and friends he had never had; he played with them and talked to them and the discovery of a new slip or seedling sent his heart soaring.

Cautiously, then, he made friends with Aunt Susan's plants. He brought water for the sweet peas and snipped faded blooms from the geraniums. Once Jim saw him cultivating the yellow doorstep roses and said, "What you doing to them flowers?"

"Loving them," George replied guilelessly.

Under his touch the roses flourished and the geraniums never yellowed. When Mrs. Fred Baynham came to visit and sighed that her roses never looked so pretty as *those*, Aunt Susan promised to send her George around. "It's all his doing," she said. "He has a magic way with growing things."

And so one summer day George climbed the rail fence and crossed the field to the Baynham place, which had once belonged to Colonel Grant. Here his mother and father had lived, and he tried to imagine them walking these very fields. But it was hard for him to conjure up the image of a mother or a father, and soon he was distracted by the big red brick house. He circled it in awe. All was still in the midday heat and it seemed to George that he was all alone in a strange land, just he and the towering house—and the roses. He found them on the northeast side and knew at once why they were so scraggly: only in the earliest hours of morning could the sun's nourishment reach them. In little more than an hour he had moved and watered them, humming his odd little song as he worked. Then he went in the back door to find Mrs. Baynham.

The kitchen, like the yard, was deserted. But the house was cool, beckoning, and unwilled, his feet moved through the dining room and the hall, and he barely breathed in the splendid silence. The walls were painted and the furniture gleamed and, standing now in the parlor door, he saw the most astounding sight of all: pictures hung around the room, beautiful pictures of forests and flowers—even the bearded old men who glared down at him seemed beautiful to George. And he went hungrily from one to the other, as though memorizing every line and color, so lost in this enchanted world that he didn't hear Mrs. Baynham until, standing right behind him, she spoke.

"Do you like the paintings, George?"

He wheeled, poised to flee. But she was smiling at him. He stuttered: "I—I . . ."

"Did you come to see about the roses?"

He found voice. "I t-took and replanted the roses, ma'am. In the s-s-sun. Roses want s-s-sun, ma'am."

"Thank you, George. Take this for your trouble."

She put a nickel in his hand and he clutched it tightly as he backed out of the room. But it was neither the nickle nor the roses he thought of as he went back across the field. His mind's eye still looked at those pictures. And that evening he squeezed the dark juice from some pokeberries and, dipping his finger in, carefully drew a circle on a flat rock. After that he was forever making pictures, scratching faces on rock with a piece of tin, or tracing the outline of a flower in any smooth place on the ground.

Meanwhile Mrs. Baynham's roses battened and bloomed and the good lady sang the praises of Carver's George wherever she went. Other neighbors came to him. "Why is my begonia dying, George?" And, "*My* roses are spotted, George—what's wrong?" And he would pick sucking mites off the roses, and water and mulch the begonia and, later, tell Aunt Susan, "They just *l-look* at their flowers. They don't *s-s-see* them, else they'd know what's wrong good as me." When a plant was far gone, he would dig it up and carry it off to his secret place in the woods, shaking the roots clean and replanting it in rich forest loam, then nursing it back to full vigor. People took to calling him the plant doctor, and for miles around it was said that Carver's George could heal the ailments of anything that grew.

He learned that petunias planted in pure loam paled, and some died. When he mixed in sand they recovered, and he decided that some plants couldn't digest so rich a diet, just as he couldn't eat too many of Aunt Susan's corn biscuits without getting a stomachache. Thereafter he tested all his plants in various combinations of loam, sand and clay. He tracked down grubs and worms that fed on roots, and got rid of them. That summer Uncle Moses fretted because his best apple tree was withering, and George crawled among the limbs until he found the one where a colony of coddling moths had made a home. "S-saw that branch off, Uncle Moses," he said, "and it'll get better." And it did.

"There ain't nothin' that boy don't know," an awed Moses Carver told his wife.

But the truth was that there were many things George didn't know. Why did bees especially love clover? And why did some bushes flower in the spring, some in autumn, and some not at all? How could a tiny seed become an eight-foot sunflower? The days weren't long enough for him to ponder all the mysteries of nature, and to a corner by the hearth he brought beetles and tobacco worms and lizards, and examined them by firelight. They were his treasures, and so were rocks and flower bulbs and the leaves of trees.

"Out!" Aunt Susan commanded regularly. "I want all those—those *things* out of the house!"

And reluctantly, mournfully, George would carry his treasures outside—and return in another day or two with a frog and a caterpillar. In the fall he brought tall stalks of milkweed into the kitchen. He wanted to see the actual opening of the swollen pods, although Aunt Susan warned that he'd be in for a switching if it messed her house. Late one afternoon, while jelly boiled on the stove and a fresh tub of butter waited to be carried to the milkhouse, George, outside, heard a sudden, unbelieving gasp and plunged through the door. Aunt Susan stood stunned, transfixed, in a sea of silky-downy floss, the milkweed pods opening with soundless regularity, and their teeming white seed, caught by the breeze from the open window, floated eerily and endlessly through the house, saturating the jelly and the butter and the water pail, and filling George with rapt astonishment.

As soon as she found voice, Aunt Susan cried out for Moses, who came to stare owl-eyed at this domestic disaster. "I want you to take this child down to the barn, sir," his wife was saying in her best no-nonsense tone. "At once!"

And the old man and the boy marched to the barn, and George, still entranced by his miracle, said, "You ought to have s-seen the pods opening. You just ought!" In the barn, he took ten brisk switch strokes across the bare bottom, then said again, "Oh, you ought to have s-seen it, Uncle Moses!"

The old man shook his head in amazement and said, "Well I guess I ought, at that." And together the two started back up to the house to help clean up.

A mile from the Carver place, in Locust Grove, there was a raw, one-room cabin that served as the community's house of worship. A preacher rode out from Neosho or Joplin to conduct the service each Sunday morning. During the week the cabin was a schoolhouse. Sometimes George would walk over there, to sit on the doorstep and listen curiously as the teacher read from a book and the children recited their lessons and sums. And one day, beyond that door, a new world suddenly beckoned him and it was filled with dreams undreamed and a vision so breathtaking that he couldn't wholly grasp its glittering promise. To learn, to be able to read, to find the answers to all his "Why's" and "How-come's . . ."

He ran most of the way home and found Moses in the field, and stammered with wild excitement. "When c-can I g-go to the s-s-school, Uncle Moses? Am I old enough? Am-am-am I?"

The old man wiped sweat from his forehead and

searched the blue sky for words. How do you crush a dream gently? How do you tell a boy bursting with his newfound hunger to learn that though the slaves were free, and though Missouri law now proclaimed that "no Negro should know any master, only God," George could *never* go to the Locust Grove school, nor to any school for white children.

"Can I go tomorrow, Uncle Moses?" the boy asked, eyes begging.

And at last Moses Carver held George's shoulders and told him no, he couldn't go tomorrow. "They don't allow colored young 'uns in that school."

"Colored young 'uns," George repeated.

He knew, of course, that he was colored. He could see it in the looking glass. But never before had it meant any more than that his face and hands were darker than Aunt Susan's, as the red roses were darker than the yellow ones. But both were roses. One wasn't any better than the other. And now, all in a sickening rush, it came to him that it was different with people, that it was better to be white than black and, stricken, lost, he went to hide himself in his secret glade. His small-boy's mind struggled with this thunderbolt, trying to sort out things he knew to be true from those that were false. In the world of nature—in which he believed so passionately—the sun shone on all plants, and the rain fell on them, and it didn't matter what color they were. That was *true*. That was *right*. How, then, could people, grownups, make such a mistake? There was no answer, and Carver's George pressed his cheek to the warm earth and wept, held by fear and a dark premonition. But he absolutely refused to abandon his dream.

Aunt Susan dug an old blue-backed speller from the

trunk she had brought from Illinois and taught him his letters. In weeks he had memorized every line in the book and, though he had no notion of what some of the words meant, he could rattle off the spelling of each. Moses taught him simple sums and guided his fist until, unaided, he could write his name. He spent hours peering through the almanac, calling out the words he recognized, groping for the meaning of sentences. Unable to stay away, he went back to the doorstep of the Locust Grove school and imagined that he was sitting at a desk inside, that his was the voice reciting the day's lesson. But it was not enough. It was never enough.

Sometimes, on a fair morning, Uncle Moses gave him some pennies and let him walk to Neosho with Jim. It was eight miles away, the county seat, and seemed to George the most hectic place in the world. Every face was strange, some of them black, like his, and he was always glad to start back home. Then he stumbled on the school for colored children.

The brothers had separated, George to look for a crochet hook, and arranged to meet on the northern edge of the town as soon as the sun dropped below the church belfry. George bought his hook and, wandering, found himself standing before a log shanty into which a straggling line of Negro youngsters was moving. When the door closed behind the last one, George pressed his ear to it—and heard the now-familiar drone of children reciting their lessons. But these were *colored children!* And this must be a *colored school!*

He fled to meet Jim, and stammered so trying to tell about his discovery that the older boy shook him. "Slow down, now! I don't hear anything but stutter."

"I c-can't help it."

"Yes you can. Just slow down."

George took a deep breath and started again: "There a s-school in Neosho, a school for the colored. And, Jim, I mean to g-go there."

They walked along the dusty country road under the paling afternoon sun. They were different as could be, one tall and rangy, and the other so thin, frail, vulnerable. Jim didn't understand his brother, not his preoccupation with that speller, nor the foolishness over flowers and things. But there had always been a closeness between them, a companionship that transcended their differences. And now Jim felt frightened for his little brother— it was such a momentous, measureless thing he contemplated—and he didn't know what to say. He scuffed the dirt and muttered, "Where you aim to stay?"

"I don't know."

Jim stopped in the road, suddenly angry. "Well, then, what's the sense of it? You got a good place. You're learning them words out of Aunt Sue's book . . ."

"I want to learn *all* the words," George said, his voice reedy and shrill, but filled with his intensity. "I want to learn enough words to *write* a book. There's lots I want to learn."

Jim stared at the younger boy for a long, searching moment, then they started walking again. It was no use, he thought. He would never understand. The only thing he knew for sure was that if George said he was going, he would go.

This much Moses Carver knew, too. "I can't stop you," he said quietly when George told him. "Wouldn't if I could. But how do you mean to live? What'll you do for food and a place to sleep?"

The boy hunched his thin shoulders, looking up at the

bearded man with eyes that betrayed him, for they missed by a wide margin, matching the braveness of his words. "I c-c-can c-c-cook and-and-and s-s-sweep . . ."

"Take your time, boy."

". . . and t-tend fires."

Moses nodded solemnly. He put his hand on George's head, and it was all settled. Aunt Susan made him some dodgers—strips of home-cured fat meat between loaves of baked corn bread—and one fall morning, sad and silent, she stood with Moses and Jim and watched the thin boy walk through the gate and out into the wide world. He carried some of his rocks and a clean shirt in a bundle over his shoulder. He seemed so terribly alone on the road, the unswerving road that ended only at the far horizon, a tiny fleck against the enormous sky. The year was 1875 and Carver's George was probably fourteen years old.

III. The Lesser Rose

THAT BOY TOLD ME HE CAME TO NEOSHO
TO FIND OUT WHAT MADE HAIL AND
SNOW, AND WHETHER A PERSON COULD
CHANGE THE COLOR OF A FLOWER BY
CHANGING THE SEED. IMAGINE! I TOLD
HIM HE'D NEVER FIND ALL THAT OUT IN
NEOSHO, NOR IN JOPLIN, EITHER, AND
MAYBE NOT EVEN IN KANSAS CITY. BUT
ALL THE TIME I KNEW HE'D FIND IT OUT
—SOMEWHERE.

—*Mariah Watkins*

Neosho had once been the Confederate capital of Missouri. Through the war Federal troops and rebels had battled in the streets, burning the courthouse and terrorizing the people. Only now, more than a decade later, was the little town beginning fully to recover from the ravages of the great rebellion. One of its three lead mines was back in production and a new flour mill had been built. The Freedmen's Bureau, that schizoid minister of the Reconstruction—half brutal corruption, half shining service to the four million emancipated, bewildered pawns of the war—had come and gone, its presence in Neosho marked by the existence of the Lincoln School for Colored Children.

Now Carver's George, who had drawn courage from his dream and the warm sun, stood outside that tumble-

27

down shack for a long time. It was empty, the door padlocked, for the sun had long since slipped down behind
the church belfry. Then, all at once, it was dark and
George felt tiny and isolated. No one in this whole town
knew he was here, or cared. He listened to the knowing
sounds of the night creatures and thought longingly of
the Carver cabin: they would be sitting by the fire now,
their bellies full, the dishes washed, and the night sounds
would be friendly in their ears.

What was he to do? Where should he go? He had only
his dream now, and he wasn't sure it would sustain him
through this first night.

He began to circle the school, shrinking from every
footfall, hungry, afraid, and never before so awfully all
alone. He climbed a fence and came to the dark hulk of
a barn. Suddenly his legs ached with fatigue and when
he found the loft door, he crawled through and burrowed
into the hay, willing himself to stop trembling. He
smelled the horses—he was friendly with horses—and in
a little while his eyes quit straining to pierce the blackness. He ate the last of the dodgers and lay back, seeing
Aunt Susan knitting and Jim poking at the last log in the
cabin fire. Then he fell asleep.

He woke chilled and tense and clambered down
through the loft door, all but lost in the early morning
mists steaming up from the ground. He ran to the schoolhouse, brushing hay from his clothes as he went, but it
was still padlocked and, aimlessly, he returned to the
barnyard, hungry all over again. There were some sunflowers by the fence and he picked seeds and sat on a
pile of kindling nibbling at them disconsolately, never
noticing a small house across the yard. Presently, though,

a wiry colored lady came out of the back door and saw
the small huddling figure on her kindling stack.

"What're you doing here?"

"Just s-s-settin'," George said.

"I can *see* that."

Hands on hips, she gazed down on him sternly and
George, scrambling to his feet, had to swallow twice, and
hard, before any sound came up from his throat. "I was-
was-was a-waitin' for the s-s-school to open."

"You got a long wait. This is Saturday."

"S-Saturday," he echoed forlornly. "I-I-I . . ."

"Oh, quit that stammering. I don't bite. Where's your
folks?"

"In D-Diamond Grove—Mr. Moses Carver and . . ."

"And you came here to go to school?"

"Yes, ma'am."

"You hungry, boy?"

"Yes, ma'am." For the first time, George noticed that
for all her snippy way of talking, her eyes were soft as
candle-shine.

"You get yourself over to that pump and scrub clean,
then come on in." She snatched up some kindling and
marched back to the house.

George stared after her for a moment, then ran to the
pump and washed his hands and face vigorously. By the
time he knocked timidly on the back door, the sweet
smell of biscuits hung in the air and in another moment,
oblivious to his surroundings, he was sloshing syrup over
their golden warmth and eating as though he had just
discovered the wonder of food.

So it was that George came to the home of Mariah
Watkins, washerwoman, midwife and possessor of a soul

so tender and bountiful that she took upon herself the
responsibility for all the stray creatures that brushed her
life. Years before she had learned to shield her heart with
that mask of sternness—without it she would have broken
down in tears at the sight of every hapless and hungry
Carver's George who crossed her path. She and her husband Andrew, a hard-working odd-jobs man, had no
children of their own, but Mariah always spoke of the
boys and girls she had delivered as "my babies," even
long after they had married and raised families of their
own. Years later, when her "babies," black and white,
gave a party for her, half the town was represented and
her street was crowded with the rigs of Neosho's first
families.

All that morning George watched nervously as Mariah
scrubbed great heaps of linen, and watched even more
nervously when her husband came home for his noon
meal and the two whispered to each other, now and then
throwing a sharp look in his direction. Then Mariah came
to him and said, "You can stay here, with us, if you'll
work."

"Oh, I'll work, ma'am," he said eagerly, almost desperately. "I'm a g-good worker, honest. I can s-s-sweep and
tend f-fires and . . ." He stopped short, then gulped:
"Can I g-go to s-s-school?"

"Of course," Mariah snapped. "That's what you came
for, isn't it?"

Andrew Watkins, grizzled and gray-headed, smiled at
him. "You call me Uncle Andy, hear. And her Aunt Mariah. We're mighty happy to have you, son."

And George said, "Thank you—both of you." Then he
turned away, for great tears were filling his eyes.

That first night, as Mariah curtained off a corner of

the one-room house to make a place for him to sleep,
George tried again to express his gratitude: "I was mighty
l-lucky, picking your yard to s-set in."

Mariah stopped what she was doing. "Luck had nothing to do with it, boy," she said crisply. "God brought you
to my yard. He has work for you, and He wants Andrew
and me to lend a hand."

"Yes'm," he whispered.

He had marched forth into the world with only the
fuzziest notion of God's function in it, but he had come
to the right place to find out. According to Mariah Watkins' simple and straightforward faith, God was everywhere; he had a plan for each of His children; He permitted nothing to happen by accident or mere chance.
Soon this truth would be an unshakable part of George's
being, as would the other two precepts by which Aunt
Mariah lived: cleanliness and work. Her cabin was immaculate, its floors covered with rag rugs and worn
smooth from countless scrubbings. It smelled of spices
and pine, and the back door looked out on a yard raked
bristling clean. Standing on a bench were the washtubs
and board with which Mariah earned her living, and decades later George had only to close his eyes to see her
again, that slight figure moving up and down over those
steaming tubs, rhythmically, laboriously, endlessly.

On Saturday he swept the floor and washed dishes and
carried in wood for the fire. And on Sunday, wearing his
clean shirt, he went to the African Methodist church with
Aunt Mariah and Uncle Andrew. He was a little frightened—he had no idea what went on inside a church—
but from Uncle Moses' bias, suspected dark incantations,
perhaps even a human sacrifice.

Someone had to stand alongside Preacher Givens and

read the scriptures for him. But when the little congrega-
tion sang their hymns, the music melted the knot of fear
in George's stomach. And when Preacher Givens began
to speak of God's love and concern for each of His children, for every one of them who sat expectant and so full
of hope in the creaking, tin-roofed structure, it seemed as
though the sun gathered strength and poured its warmth
over him. He wanted to cry with the mysterious stirrings
inside him, the gladness. It was a feeling he had learned
to count on every Sunday when he went to church with
the Watkins, and ever after when he entered God's house.

As George was climbing the fence on his way to school
Monday morning, Mariah called to him from the back
door: "You can't go calling yourself Carver's George any
more! You're a person, hear? From now on you're George
Carver."

"Yes'm," he said, and strange as the name sounded on
his tongue, he so reported himself to the teacher, a young
and fidgety Negro named Stephen S. Frost. Then he
went to squeeze into a place on the back bench.

Nearly 75 pupils were packed tight in the tiny schoolhouse, some of them smaller than George, and some almost as big as grownups. George concentrated very hard
on Mr. Frost's every word, mindless of the distractions. A
constant undertone of sound buzzed through the room,
regularly punctuated by a fit of coughing. Whenever
someone crossed a leg or shifted in his seat, all the others
on that bench had to move, too. And the air soon grew
fetid, thick with the smell of breathing and too many
bodies pressed too close. In winter the wind would come
knifing through every chink in the walls and, except for
the handful of children next to the wood stove, everyone

wore their coats and mittens the day long, and still shivered with cold.

None of this mattered to George. He was in school. He had his own book, a first reader, and a piece of slate to write on, and at noon recess that first day he scrambled over the fence and exploded into the house to proudly display them to Aunt Mariah. He gobbled his lunch, and threading through the games and confusion in the schoolyard, was waiting at the front door long before Mr. Frost summoned the others back to class with his bell.

The day—and all the next days—sped by for George. When he wasn't at school, he had his reader propped in front of him, even when he washed dishes or helped Aunt Mariah scrub clothing. Sometimes, in the schoolyard, the other children coaxed him into a game of crack-the-whip or run-sheep-run. Almost invariably, though, he wound up with skinned knees and felt foolish at his clumsiness. Shy, cowed by all the shouting and stomping, he tried to lose himself in a quiet corner, drawing pictures on his slate, biding time until the school bell rang.

It was a pattern that was to repeat itself all through George Carver's life. Solitude seemed to be his destiny, and he was never happier than when he could be alone and at work. Aunt Mariah taught him to iron—"Mind what you're about now. It has to be just so for my customers!"—and, the inevitable reader opened alongside a mountain of freshly-washed clothing, he ironed contentedly through to the last handkerchief.

One day in mid-November, George ventured uptown and stood until nearly dark outside the ladies' wear shop, studying the intricately crocheted cuffs and collar on a handsome dress. Then he went home and, pretending he was only idling, hiding his work each night, he repro-

"Yes'm," Jim said.

"Seeing it's near dinnertime, you might as well eat with us tonight."

As soon as she had gone back into the house, the brothers danced around each other one more time, then climbed up and sat on the fence to talk. How were Uncle Moses and Aunt Sue? George wanted to know. And what had decided Jim on coming to town?

Jim said he had thought about it all winter, then made up his mind that he would have a try at going to school, too. "If you think it's so all-fired important, it must be." He nudged George slyly, "You finding the answers to all your questions about the seeds and the flowers?"

George looked at the schoolhouse, and at the darkening sky beyond. "No," he answered, "not yet." Then turning back to Jim, he said, "But I c-can read now, and write, and pretty s-soon you will, too, Jim."

But it turned out differently. Jim was not cut out to be a student and after only a short time he quit Mr. Frost's class to learn the plastering trade. George was disappointed, but Jim, as outgoing as his little brother was timid, fit smoothly into the Negro community in Neosho and was happy as could be.

Meanwhile, George sought out occasional odd jobs around town and zealously hoarded the pennies he earned. When the Slaters went to St. Louis for a visit, he minded their house, reporting each evening to Aunt Mariah that he had fixed the screen door and polished the lamp and hauled the fireplace ashes until, at last, she brought him up short: "Boy, it's time you learned that I don't care, and Mrs. Slater don't care, and nobody cares, how *many* things you've done. The only thing that counts is how *well* you've done them!"

Another winter came and again George was sniffling and coughing all the time, sapped by an unending weariness that kept him home from school for days. Not that that mattered now—he had long since learned all there was to learn in Mr. Frost's class. But he could not believe that it was God's plan for him to be scrawny and sick all his life. Maybe if he went somewhere else—like one of those ailing plants he'd transplanted in his secret glade—maybe then he would grow and get better. Maybe he'd find a school to go to. Maybe the answers to all his questions were waiting for him in some faraway place, and all he had to do was search it out.

In December he heard that the Smiths down the street were moving to Fort Scott in Kansas, nearly 75 miles away. Was that the place for him? Free Kansas, they'd once called it, and the name still had a fine ring to it. It symbolized equality, opportunity. Were his answers there, in the great open West? For days he struggled with his small-boy fears and his passionate longing to learn, to know. Then, gathering his courage, he knocked on the Smiths' door.

Would they take him along to Fort Scott? he asked. He would be no trouble. He would bring his own food and help with the mules. And they agreed.

In those last hectic days he and Jim had their photograph taken together—both in ruffled shirts and trousers that looked far too big for them, both solemn-faced—and tramped over the frozen road to Diamond Grove so George could bid good-bye to the Carvers. From Mr. Frost he got a certificate of merit dated December 22, 1876. And on a biting cold January morning, George Carver hauled his little parcel up on a cluttered wagon, up among the bedsteads and the pots and pans, and turned to wave to Jim and the Watkins. Bundled to the ears, he looked like a small boy, though he must have been sixteen, tiny, fragile, dark eyes glistening wide in a slit of a face. But there was in those eyes, Aunt Mariah could see, a certain resolve, a spunkiness that had not been there when he first came to her.

"Get him a good school, Lord," she prayed softly. "Get him a teacher who's right smart because, Lord, there's an awful lot that boy wants to know."

"Giddap!" Mr. Smith bellowed. And the mules ambled off.

It was a long journey. The road wound west through the Ozarks, then north across the broad and empty plain. When the mules tired, George and the family took turns walking, the lashing wind tearing at their faces and, sometimes, furious swirls of snow penning them in a white vastness whose limits could not even be imagined. By night they huddled close to the campfire, eating numbly, silently, then curling into a shivering half-sleep. On the fourth day the wagon clattered up to the Marmaton River and turned into Fort Scott. On the main street, a bustling, cobbled thoroughfare, George slid down from his perch and, clasping his bundle, watched the Smiths move off until the wagon disappeared around a distant corner. He was alone again.

A horse galloped by, the rider swearing at the forlorn figure in the center of the road and reining hard to avoid running him down. Shakily George retreated to the wood sidewalk, walking slowly, irresolutely, toward the big hotel by the stagecoach depot. People brushed by him, all in a terrible hurry, and once, when he steeled himself to ask a colored lady if she knew where a boy might find work, she responded with a sort of explosive, "Hah!" and rushed on past him.

He shrank close to the storefronts and slunk down the next side street he came to. For a long time he just wandered, the lump of dread within him so sharply defined that he felt as though he could finger it. Not until the bleak winter sky darkened could he force himself up to those forbidding kitchen doors, stammering out his sad little message: did the lady of the house need someone to sweep floors and tend fires? Some told him no, politely; some looked at him without really seeing him and slammed the door closed; and finally one said that the lady across the street, Mrs. Payne, was looking for help.

The house was enormous, shiny white, enclosed by meticulous banks of dark shrubbery. Again George knocked, trying to stand tall out of his coat, hating himself for being so puny, and practicing the words under his breath so he wouldn't stutter when the door opened.

"They said you needed someone to do-do-do housework." He pointed vaguely across the street.

Mrs. Payne was tall and straight and had tight black hair. "I was looking for a girl," she said briskly, but didn't close the door.

"I can s-sweep and wash d-d-dishes and—and everything."

She regarded him with obvious doubt. "Can you cook?"

"Oh, yes, ma'am! I can make . . ."

"Come in out of the cold."

A warm, welcoming fire burned in the kitchen. The hearty smell of roasting beef reached out to George, enveloped him and made him suddenly light-headed with hunger and fatigue. He wondered if he dared lean against the wall, then decided not. He concentrated fiercely on replying to Mrs. Payne's barrage of questions without stammering into fatal incomprehensibility: what was his name? where had he come from? how did he happen to learn housework? how much had he done?

Abruptly, then, she said, "All right, I'll give you a try. You can start with dinner. We'll have that meat and a bread pudding, biscuits—you'll find everything you need in the cupboard—apple pie and coffee. My husband is *especially* fussy about his coffee. We'll eat promptly at six."

With that, she whirled and vanished beyond a swinging door and George Carver, stunned, unstrung by the enormity of his task, gaped after her weakly. He hadn't meant to lie. He *could* cook—in a way. He had boiled collard greens and eggs for Aunt Mariah, and even fried bacon. But biscuits and pudding and pie—these were as alien to him as Mrs. Payne's gleaming stove and the mystifying array of cutlery and dishes laid out on the sideboard. What was he to do?

Trapped, he hung his coat and washed up at the pump —he had never even *seen* an indoor pump. Then he opened the cupboard and took down flour, potatoes, coffee, staring at them dispirited, wondering if he should throw himself on Mrs. Payne's mercy or try to brazen it out long enough to capture for himself one slice of that succulent beef. And it was at that moment that Mrs. Payne came back to the kitchen.

"George . . ." she began.

"Ma'am," he blurted.

They looked at each other, George's breath caught in his throat and his brain reeling in desperate, tumbling confusion.

"Yes?" Mrs. Payne prompted.

And from some last uncontaminated wellspring of common sense, he dredged up the wit to say, "Excuse me for interrupting, Ma'am, but I do want everything to be j-just right this first time, and if you could show me exac-exac-exactly how you like everything p-pre-pared . . ."

"Hmm," she said. "Yes. Well, we'd best start with the biscuits. I use two cups of flour and about so much baking powder . . ."

George watched her raptly, his trap-like mind clamping down on every word she uttered, his hands secretly aping hers through the mixing and whipping and ladling procedures. When the biscuits were baking, he tucked *that* recipe away in a corner of his brain and applied himself to the mysteries of bread pudding, a dish he'd never so much as heard of before.

The pie required so many apples, Mrs. Payne said, and so much cinnamon, and her coffee turned out best when she used six teaspoonsful and no more than half a pot of water.

When she finally left him alone, he mumbled the separate proportions aloud to himself again and again as he worked, dancing from hearth to stove to oven in frantic determination to ward off culinary disaster that seemed imminent. Miraculously, though, dinner was on the table when the master of the house, a plumply genial man, returned home, and ear pressed to the swinging door, George heard not a murmur of complaint. He had done it!

Before too many days passed he was enriching the biscuit batter with an extra egg, flavoring the meat with a few shreds of bay leaf and otherwise flexing his imag-

ination—with the most astonishing results. By the time
the month was out he had won a bread- and biscuit-
making contest at the Methodist church. Each evening
around five o'clock, one or more of the neighborhood
ladies dropped in to visit, and though they chattered
away with Mrs. Payne, their eyes remained fixed on
every move George made at the stove, nor could they
ever be persuaded to leave the kitchen. And—supreme
accolade!—one night at dinner Mr. Payne boomed out
to his wife in a voice that could be heard throughout the
house, "My compliments, Madam. Your new cook is a
jewel!"

Often, when his work was done and the kitchen shining clean, George would lie in his tiny room beneath the
back steps and listen to Mrs. Payne play the piano. And
the music seemed somehow to suggest all the learning
in all the books he'd never read, to imply questions he
didn't yet know enough to ask, and he would fall asleep
with the melody in his ears and a nagging urgency in
his breast. He had not come to Fort Scott to be a cook.
It was only a job, useful for staving off hunger and cold,
but no substitute for school. He must permit neither
prizes nor praise to divert him from finding out all the
things he had to know. He must hurry!

He left the Paynes in early spring, having saved every
cent of his wages, and presented himself for enrollment
at the big brick school on the square. There were long
corridors and many rooms, and George felt himself to
be the focus of every eye as he hurried along with his
newly-purchased books, shoes squeaking and trousers
threatening to slide down on his narrow hips. Once inside the classroom, though, he was oblivious to every-

thing but what he could learn. He struggled with geography and arithmetic, subjects scarcely mentioned by Mr. Frost, did well at reading and spelling, and again commanded his classmates' attention—envious, this time, awed—in nature study: he knew every rock and flower and seed, and he asked questions even the teacher couldn't answer.

He had found a place to stay by the stagecoach depot, a decrepit cabin that cost him a dollar a week. He spent not more than that for food and not a penny on anything else. All afternoon he studied and, at night, by a single candle, read everything he could lay his hands on—books, circulars, old newspapers, pamphlets. On Sunday, when the sun was warm enough, he walked off into the woods and self-conscious, needing the silent encouragement of the things he loved best in all the world, he drew their pictures: a slender birch, a rabbit contemplating him with curiosity but no fear, the eager young wildflowers of spring.

Frugal as George was, his money barely lasted until summer, then he had to go to work again. This time he found a job at the hotel, Wilder House, scrubbing sheets and pillowcases, his chin barely clearing the top of the great tub, but his arms pumping furiously. Later he washed and ironed the linen of ranchers and businessmen who came in on the stagecoach from Kansas City. By September, he had enough money put by to go back to school.

And so it went, the weeks of work to pay for his snatches of education, and the learning nourishing him, arming him with the heart to labor on. He was often lonely, older and a world apart from his classmates, almost all of whom were white, and he was sometimes afraid. Though Kansas had been free, Fort Scott was a wartime enclave of Southern sympathy, and even now the racial fires smouldered. Once, looking at some pictures in a store window, George had been accosted by two white men:

"Hey, boy, where'd you get them books?"

"I bought them, sir. At school."

One of them laughed forbiddingly, "Hear that, Pete? He says he bought 'em at school."

"Since when they lettin' niggers into school?" the other snarled, his pig eyes narrowed to dark, glowering slits. "I say he stole 'em."

Common sense told George to run. He felt sure he could dart between them and be gone before they collected their wits. But something else held him fast, his back to the storefront and his face turned to the antagonists in tranquil acceptance of what had to come. He had done nothing wrong. He did not want to be bullied into running. That was more important, even, than his books.

"Hand 'em over!"

"They're mine, sir," George said.

They moved more quickly than he thought they could. One hit him on the side of the head with a clenched fist, and even as he slid toward the ground, dazed and despairing, the other snatched the books from his fingers. Then they walked deliberately down the street. And though there were many passersby, no one stopped them. No one said a word.

George wandered the back streets for a long time, not caring where he was, only thinking about what he was going to do. He would be unable to go back to school for he had no money to buy new books. Dark dreams assailed his sleep that night and dogged his next days. Eventually he went to work for a colored blacksmith, sweeping the stable and delivering freshly-shod horses, but he kept to himself and rarely spoke. Then the shock of horror tore wide the wound of his spirit.

Late one afternoon, returning to the blacksmith shop, he saw a sullen crowd pressing on the wood jail and felt suddenly, hopelessly, trapped by their shrill cries. He clung to the shadows on the far side of the street but could not will his feet to flee. Some men had built a great bonfire in the square. Others were pounding on the jail-house door.

"Drag him out!" they screamed. "Let's get him!"

And they did. A wild-eyed wedge of mob thundered through the door and the screams soared to a shriek, an agonized cry for vengeance and blood. A moment more and a pleading, terrified Negro was flung out at their feet. The men cursed incoherently as they beat him and kicked him, and the women held their children high to see this human sacrifice to hatred and heedless passion.

"Please! Please!" the prisoner begged.

"Nigger!" his executioners shouted back, as though that were the charge against him, the evidence and the verdict. Then they drenched him with oil and dragged him, bleeding and still begging, to the square and threw him into the leaping flames. George saw him try once, twice, to pull himself erect. Then, blazing, a look of utter despair on his face, he fell back into the fire and was still.

All through the night George saw that look and heard the piteous plea for mercy and tried to wipe the stench of burning flesh from his nostrils. And long before dawn, still trembling, he gathered his belongings and fled Fort Scott forever.

A long time afterward, George Carver would write of this time in his life, "Sunshine was profusely intermingled with shadows, such as are naturally cast on a defenseless orphan by those who wish to prey upon him."

If the closed door of the schoolhouse at Locust Grove had taught him the burden of a black skin, the lynching at Fort Scott unmasked its peril, and for a long time this solemn truth festered in his consciousness. He knew now that anyone else was free to search out his destiny along the broadest highways, but that he would have to keep to the side roads. He knew that at any time, by reason of blind bitterness, or pretext, or even whim, he could be smashed into oblivion and no one would care and perhaps not even notice. He knew that if he reached his place in the sun it would be a miracle. But he kept walking.

For ten years he wandered the western country, moving from place to place, doing odd jobs, heading for the nearest school and staying until the school could teach him no more, starting a grade in one town and finishing it in another. And wherever he went, three eternal needs went with him: where would he sleep? who would feed him? how could he pay for the next set of schoolbooks?

He cooked, scrubbed clothes, chopped wood, tended gardens, cleaned rugs, dug ditches, picked fruit, hammered nails, swabbed outhouses, whitewashed fences— whatever anyone wanted done. Once, in September, he came to a great wheat field and stood watching as the reaper, pulled by four horses, felled the graceful yellow shocks. A man, following behind, would scoop up an armful of loose wheat, deftly tie a stalk around it and leave behind a neat bundle. Instinctively George's hands began going through the farmer's motions. Soon he was in the field walking beside him. The man squinted with surprise at the sudden appearance of the gangling boy, then gawked in amazement as the boy went through the intricate manipulations of binding. Before dark George had mastered a new skill, and all that harvest season he hired out from farm to farm, content to walk along behind the whirring reaper the day long, binding wheat under the Indian summer sun.

He roamed on, west almost to Denver, south, then back to Kansas—Paola, Olathe, Minneapolis—and on to the towns and villages of Iowa, always among strangers, never sure of anything except that *this* was the year he was going to finish the seventh grade. He tried to stay in touch with his brother Jim, but was rarely in one place long enough for a letter to catch up with him. There were days when he daydreamed of finding his mother and sister in some remote hamlet. Seldom, though, did he ever even see a colored face.

All at once, it seemed, he had grown to a gaunt six feet, bony and taut and a little stooped over from unending toil and having sometimes not enough to eat. And though he almost never stuttered any more, his voice remained as piping high as a girl's. Often, as he trudged the dusty roads, he wore his shoes around his neck to preserve them.

In Newton, Iowa, he worked in a greenhouse and basked in the daily presence of growing things. Then the owner's son accused "that nigger" of stealing his pocketknife, and George moved on. Once, beyond the gates of a great mansion, he saw a magnificent bed of roses by a pond and asked the gardener if he could come in and draw a picture of it. But some boys came along and claimed that he had invaded private property. They tore up his picture and threw him in the pond and laughed feverishly at his fumbling, desperate efforts to save himself from drowning.

One summer he signed on as the cook's helper in a railroad construction gang. Then, in the foothills of the Rockies, he joined a group of migrants and picked fruit all the way into New Mexico. All day the sun was a fierce fireball over the empty, endless land, but crisp winds cooled the night and George slept deeply, gratefully.

Walking in the desert, he came on a plant unlike any he had ever seen. It rose abruptly from the arid sand, tall and bristling with needled spears and a pale waxen bloom. He made a careful sketch of it on a crumpled scrap of paper, and nearly fifteen years later his painting of the giant *Yucca gloriosa* was to win a prize at the World's Columbian Exposition in Chicago.

Wherever he was he always woke in the hour before dawn and walked alone in God's garden. With the sun's first light he would be searching the woods and the hills, seeking nothing special but entranced by everything that grew and scampered and was. He studied the black in the forest loam and the red in a field of clay and the dazzling blue of a hillside, and he thought that if only he could take those colors from the ground he could make paintings more glorious than men had ever made before.

Somewhere in his rovings he bought an ancient accordion. With typical stubborn patience, he taught himself to play it, calling back the haunting refrains that had drifted to his back room from Mrs. Payne's piano, and recreating them on the wheezing instrument, saddened and strengthened by the poignant promise of *Swing Low, Sweet Chariot* and *Nearer, My God, To Thee.* There was beauty and goodness in this seemingly callous world, he decided. There was a God who would not forsake any of His children. And George knew then that he must keep moving and trying and praying. And somewhere . . .

In Olathe, Kansas, George had a good home with a barber. He was permitted to do his chores after classes, and so moved industriously through the sixth grade and made a good start on the seventh. Then the barber and his family left town and George went to live with an elderly Negro couple, Christopher and Lucy Seymour. They were to have a profound influence on his life.

Like Mariah Watkins, Aunt Lucy was a washerwoman, but specialized in fancy work—men's shirts starched and ironed to the rigid glaze of porcelain, fussy dresses of fragile organdy and fluted laces, ruffled, flounced and embroidered, so that a whole half day of meticulous ironing went into each one. Aunt Lucy had been owned by a Virginia family and greatly valued breeding and manners. Each shirt front and dress was for her a labor of love, a tangible token of gentility on the raw Kansas frontier, and it was a long time before she allowed George to help her. But with his first try he ironed a petticoat to precisely the required stiffness—it had to stand by itself —and she pronounced a grudging approval: "It'll do." Next day she let him iron a dress, peering nervously over his shoulder the whole time he worked.

Uncle Seymour was intensely religious. Each Sunday, morning and afternoon, he went to services in the Presbyterian church and was quietly gratified when George asked to accompany him. Evenings he sat listening in wonder and thanksgiving as the tall boy who had come to them like the answer to an unspoken prayer read from his worn leather Bible. George became Presbyterian then and remained one the rest of his life. "At least I never heard that they threw me out," he would later say with a small smile. But the fact was that denominations meant little to him. If the door of a church—any church—was open, he went in.

In 1880 the Seymours journeyed west to Minneapolis, Kansas, a growing, bustling little town in the Solomon River valley. Here George could have a chance to go to a proper high school. The family moved into a bare two-room shack with great gaps between the wall planks, which George promptly weatherstripped. Then he white-washed the entire house and hung out a handsomely-lettered sign: "Fine Laundry."

The school was a sturdy new building, grades one to eight divided among its first three rooms, and all the high school classes crowded into the fourth. But it was a high school. Every morning George walked toward that fourth room, that temple of higher learning, pretending that it was his destination, turning off only at the last minute toward his own seventh grade class. He was well past twenty, he knew, and had at least another year of schooling before he could qualify for the high school courses. But the dream danced plainly and everlastingly in his eyes and nothing, not the passing years nor the curious looks the other students cast at their gangling, overgrown classmate, discouraged him.

Before long it became apparent that Aunt Lucy could never cope with all the laundry that came to her door.

As word of the new washerwoman's skill spread, young clerks brought her their boiled shirts, and the ladies of prospering farmers and businessmen brought their fancy dresses, and soon, instead of returning everything in a day or two, Aunt Lucy still had the same stacks in her baskets a week later. So it was that with her blessing and encouragement young George Carver first went into business for himself.

His establishment was a one-room cabin with a kitchen lean-to in a draw below the business street. It was reached by a series of plank bridges and carefully-emplaced rock steps. Soon, though, a steady stream of customers was picking a way down the hill. "George Carver's Laundry" was a success from the outset.

For the first time George had friends. The amusement he'd first roused among his young classmates had given way to admiration for his enormous fund of information, and gratefulness for his willingness to coach them over rough spots in arithmetic and nature study. They took to walking down to the draw in the afternoon and oohed and aahed over George's paintings and his collection of rocks and pressed wildflowers. He would tell them stories out of his wanderings, or read to them from a propped-open book as he ironed, and by the time the class moved on to the high school room, unassuming George Carver would have won a "Best-Liked Boy" election hands down.

Gathering confidence, he buckled on his accordion and led school marches, a long black coat whipping at his shoetops with each stride, elbows wagging as he pumped away vigorously. He played for Friday night get-togethers—"Play *Yankee Doodle*, George!" they called eagerly. "Play *Long Ago*." He even plunged into local

dramatics and, for all his lanky height, was usually assigned the part of a girl, his high voice and a genuine
talent weaving the necessary illusion.

It was around this time that he took on a middle name.
There was another George Carver in Minneapolis and
sometimes letters meant for George didn't reach him.
Finally he picked a middle initial at random and, once,
when asked jokingly if the "W" stood for Washington,
grinned and said, "Why not?" But he never signed himself so. It was always "George W. Carver," or plain
"George Carver," for even in later years, when he was
most often referred to by all three names, he felt there
would be something vainglorious in his use of that middle one.

In his last winter of high school, a short, painstakingly-
printed letter came from Aunt Mariah. His brother Jim,
she wrote, had died of smallpox the summer before and
was buried in Seneca, Missouri. She would have let him
know before but had herself only just found it out. She
wished him love.

For a long silent time George sat with the letter in one
hand and, in the other, the photograph he and Jim had
had made in Neosho seven years before. There they were
gazing back at him, two dressed-up country boys, solemn
but unafraid as they made ready to march off in pursuit
of their separate stars. And now Jim, with those big
hands and that robust, straightforward way—Jim, who
had never been sick—was dead. Finally, then, the tears
came and for a little while George felt desperately alone.
But even in his sadness he knew that now, more than
ever, for Jim as well as for himself, he had to find his
star.

Suddenly the star seemed to be shining bright, beckoning him to a place called Highland in the northeast corner of Kansas. A small Presbyterian college there had weighed his application through endlessly anxious weeks —did he have enough mathematics? were his English composition courses adequate—and on a fine June morning just before graduation the postmaster finally responded to George's daily inquiry with a smile and a nod. Like a passport to heaven the long envelope came sliding toward him through the wicket.

His grades were satisfactory, the letter said. Highland College would be happy to have him in attendance commencing with the fall semester, September 20, 1885. It was signed by the Reverend Duncan Brown, D.D., Principal.

Young George Carver went on to his classes that day with a great gladness swelling in him, a sense of expectancy and early fulfillment, and all that summer he walked in the warmth of that promise. The wandering years were over; he was bound at last for a place where *all* his questions would be answered, and where—most significant question of all!—he would learn what God intended him to do with the knowledge he had accumulated in schools whose number he couldn't remember and from teachers whose faces had long blurred in his mind's eye.

He left Minneapolis before the graduation exercises. He had much to do, a long way yet to travel, before September 20. The Seymours bid him Godspeed with pride and sorrow and George turned first toward Kansas City. Never one to waste precious days, he had decided to spend the summer studying typing and shorthand at a business academy started by a high school classmate. Again he was arming himself with new tools: these were bound to be helpful at Highland and along whatever paths he was to pursue his destiny. Calculating his modest hoard of money to the last nickel, he bought a typewriter, an ungainly rig of a machine that clacked and groaned, and in the oppressive heat of the city summer, he practiced with grim, single-minded concentration. By August he had a job in the Union Depot telegraph office, typing messages from 6 P.M. until midnight.

At the end of the month he took a train to Joplin, bound south on a sentimental journey to the places of his boyhood. In Seneca he stood a long time by Jim's grave. "Born 1859," the plain wood marker said. "Died 1883." And George thought how little that told of the buoyant days that were Jim's, of his earthy aims and earthly dreams, all cut short by God's greater plan.

He walked the 13 miles to Neosho and bade a last farewell to the Watkins, then on to Diamond Grove for a nostalgic visit with the Carvers. Past seventy, Uncle Moses still worked the fields, but Aunt Susan had turned frail and far-eyed and seldom left the house. George told them of the places he had been and the things he had seen, and they listened silently, pridefully. Then Aunt Susan, fearing for him, worried that in the seeds of his aspirations lay the fruit of frustration and pain, said, "But college, George—don't you have enough learning?"

"No man has *enough* learning, Aunt Sue," he replied softly, and smiled. "And me—I'm still trying to find out what makes it rain and why sunflowers grow so tall."

For four nights he slept in his mother's cabin. On the fifth night, September 20, he was on a train clattering north toward Highland, using almost the last of his money to pay for the ticket. He was unconcerned. He would find work in Highland—he had always found work. And when he stepped down there, the platform and the depot and the whole town seemed to him to glow in the glorious autumn sun. Highland echoed his zeal, sang with promise, and he walked eagerly toward the solid red college buildings.

He had to wait a long time to see the principal. Then, in the cool stillness of that inner office, surrounded by books and dark, polished furniture, George said, "I am George W. Carver, sir."

"Yes?"

"I've come to enroll at Highland. Your letter said . . ."

"There has been a mistake."

A remembered cold touched George Carver's heart. He looked at the sad and pinched face of the Reverend Duncan Brown, D.D., trying to meet his eyes, failing, groping for words and finding only lame half-sentences: "Your letter said—I have it here . . ."

"I don't care what it said," the principal replied, unable to soften the blow, though he would perhaps have wanted to, and painfully aware that, whatever his own convictions, the trustees would never permit a black man in their school. "You didn't tell me you were Negro. Highland College does not take Negroes."

The warm and hopeful sun paled as it circled west and a sharp wind blustered down on the railroad depot and foretold the imminence of winter. George huddled on a bench. He didn't feel any wind, only hurt. He had sat so for hours, motionless, seeing nothing and hearing only the persistent echo of the principal's words: "You didn't tell me you were Negro. Highland College does not take Negroes."

He hated himself for feeling shamed—what had he done to be ashamed of? He hated himself for hating back. And finally, as the sky turned gray and he was forced to face the night and the next day, he hated himself because he had to stay in this place when his heart and mind screamed to get away. He had only a few coins in his pocket. Highland, where his dream had been bludgeoned and his soul ground down, Highland would have to be his home until he earned enough to leave it.

And then where would he go? What glimmering vision would draw him on? He was a bankrupt, as drained of hope as he was of money. Always before, no matter how mountainous the obstacles in his way, he had persevered and plowed through. He had been hungry and sick and it hadn't mattered, for he was aiming at a star. Now, in one agonizing and irredeemable moment, someone had snuffed out his star, and as he rose from the bench, stiff and weary, he looked into an unrelenting darkness. Despairing, bound, he walked toward it.

He slept that night in a barn and, in the morning, found work with a family named Beeler who ran a fruit farm just south of the town. He cooked and mended fences and pruned trees. The Beelers, a warm and congenial household, tried to draw him into their circle of friendliness. And, in fact, George did go to church with them, and played his accordion at socials and gatherings. But he was only biding time, slowly, stoically, garnering a new grubstake and trying to piece together his shattered emotions.

Meanwhile he listened thoughtfully as the family read aloud the letters of young Frank Beeler who had gone west to homestead on the Kansas plains. The Government had opened the land for settlement eight years before and now people by the hundreds were moving into what frontiersmen called the Great American Desert. Frank wrote that there was opportunity for anyone who would work. He had opened a store at a trail crossing in Ness County and now it was a town, named after himself.

And there George went in 1886, filing on a 160-acre homestead two miles south of Beeler on November 20. He recorded his age as twenty-three, but the best evidence is that he was actually past twenty-five.* With Frank Beeler's assistance, he built a sod house, cutting the virgin buffalo grass into long, brick-like strips, alternating layers as the walls rose. Across the top went a ridgepole and logs, then more sod. Dried, trimmed and whitewashed, the soddy made a warm, snug shelter, and given George's skilled hands and patient attention to detail, his was among the most substantial in the district. Soon he was first to be called when newcomers came and began to build their soddies.

Waiting to plant his spring crop, he hired out to work on a nearby stock farm. Here he passed that first terrible winter. Furious blizzards shrieked down from the north, the snow so dense that a man had to cling to a lifeline to go from house to barn. When summer came the corn shriveled in the scorching winds. There was no rain, no shade, only the everlastingly open prairie, its

---

* Robert P. Fuller, Historian at the George Washington Carver National Monument in Diamond, Missouri, has, from available evidence, deduced the likelihood that Dr. Carver was born on July 12, 1861.

emptiness accented by an occasional lonely cottonwood
on the far horizon. Buzzards soared in the big sky and
rattlesnakes basked on the rocks and rises.

For almost two years George fought the blizzards and
the burning sun. In a garden by his house he had coaxed
an array of flowers from the sod, and somehow preserved them through the winter in a sort of lean-to conservatory on the south side. Visitors would burst in from
the blinding cold and open frozen eyelids to see his win-
dowsill and table astonishingly bright with bloom. In
the long evenings he crocheted, or sorted the stones and
Indian relics he collected on long, rambling walks.

There was a huge, dome-like swelling on his land.
Time and again he covered its length and breadth,
studying the soil, poking into it, puzzling over this
freakish phenomenon of geology. "Someday they'll discover something under that dome," he once told Frank
Beeler. "I don't know enough to figure out what, but
there's something—and a lot of it—under there." The
"something" turned out to be oil, discovered half a century later. And to this day a producing well pumps
away on the original Carver homestead, the only one
within a 40-mile radius.

The passing seasons and the solitude gradually healed
George's wounded spirit. He began to read again, and
to paint, and he came to believe that, unchecked, self-
pity would grow into a wasteful, destructive force.
Though the prairie was right for some, it had become
a hiding place for him, and he didn't want to hide any
more. Unsure of what he *did* want—except the thing
that now seemed unattainable—he mused over a vague
notion that perhaps he could start a greenhouse or
nursery back East somewhere. He would have then, at
least, the company of the living, growing things he loved

and knew best. Around this time, one verse in a long, contemplative poem he wrote revealed his strengthening outlook:

O! Sit not down nor idly stand;
There's plenty to do on every hand.
If you cannot prosper in work like some,
You've at least one talent, improve that one.

In the early summer of 1888, he mortgaged his homestead for $300 and started east. Almost to the Missouri border, he turned away, ashamed somehow to return so to his native state after all his lofty talk about college. Walking north, he crossed into Iowa, scrubbing clothes in towns and hamlets along the way until, not far from Des Moines, he came to a green and peaceful village called Winterset. Here he found a job as cook at the Schultz Hotel, and here, one Sunday morning at the Baptist church, he was befriended by a medical doctor, John Milholland, and his wife. They had been attracted by his clear high tenor voice during services, and perhaps by his obvious loneliness as he sat, the only Negro, a little apart from the white congregation, and, afterwards, Mrs. Milholland, the choir director, sent her husband to invite George to their home. A long-stifled need to talk, to be with people, overcame caution, and George went, a decision for which he would ever have cause to be grateful.

The Milholland house was handsomely furnished and thickly carpeted, but George had eyes only for the magnificent piano. And when Mrs. Milholland played, memories flooded over him, and the old daydreams sprang to life, and he had to turn away to hide the powerful feelings exposed on his face. They moved into the study for

tea, and there in a corner stood an easel and palette and
a rather lifeless picture of a violet jimsonweed.

"You paint!" George said, moved anew by this second community of interests.

"I try," Mrs. Milholland replied with a wry smile. "But
as you can see my flowers turn out so stilted and wishy-
washy."

"That's because you've painted them from too far
away. And the color needs some emphasis. Here . . ."
Unable to contain his enthusiasm, George dabbed some
paint on the palette and, with a few bold brush strokes,
shortened the perspective and suddenly endowed the
jimsonweed with a certain vibrant grace.

"Say, that's pretty good!" Dr. Milholland exclaimed.
"You ought to get this young fellow to give you some
lessons, Helen."

Mrs. Milholland's eyes kept straying back to her
transformed picture, and there was wonderment and
longing in her look. "Would you, George?" she asked.
Before he could answer, though, she sat down facing
him and, all business, said, "If you will teach me to
paint I will give you singing lessons. You have a lovely
voice, and with a little training . . . well, who knows?"

George's heart leaped. He had to speak very slowly to
be sure he wouldn't stammer. "I'd be honored, Ma'am."

And thereafter, three or four afternoons each week, he
came to the Milholland house, and before long it was as
much a home as he had ever had. When the singing and
painting instructions were finished, he played the piano,
or sat in the study reading books from the doctor's substantial library. He told stories to the two young Milholland children and, in hardly any time at all, had
brought order and new beauty to the once haphazard

flower garden. He spent holidays with the Milhollands, and long evenings of song and absorbing conversation, and in the warmth of their friendship shed the last of the old Fort Scott and Highland specters. Ignorance, he decided, not hate, was his antagonist, and as long as there were people like Dr. and Mrs. Milholland, he was not alone. He had allies—and hope.

One Sunday evening, when the children had been put to bed, he even found the courage to tell them about that shattering moment in Reverend Brown's office. "George," Dr. Milholland had said, "Helen and I have been talking about what's to become of you. You've too fine a mind to remain a cook or a laundryman forever."

"I had some thoughts about starting a greenhouse," George said.

"We had some thoughts about your going to college," the doctor came back.

There was a silence. George kneaded his fingers. "I tried it once," he finally said, then told them of the dream he had carried so tenderly to Highland, and the bottomless hurt with which he'd taken its wreckage away.

"How awful!" Mrs. Milholland breathed, feeling his hurt.

But the doctor would not be put off. "That was a long time ago. You mustn't allow it to ruin your life." There was another college, he said, Simpson, in Indianola, a town not far from there. It had been endowed by a Methodist bishop, Matthew Simpson, a friend of Lincoln, and a fervent believer in the equality of all men. "They will take you in there, George—this next semester—if you have the heart to try it."

George closed his eyes, remembering his dream, his

star. "I don't know," he said very quietly. He looked at
his dear friends and wondered if, indeed, he had the
heart to walk away from the warm, protective circle of
their goodwill, to strike out one more time on that lonely
and endless path toward an unknown star. "I don't
know," he said again.

But now the dream was never out of his mind. He had
quit his job at the hotel to start a laundry and still owed
a substantial sum on his property. He would never earn
enough to pay it back by September, whispered the
small voice of self-doubt.

"You will never go at all if you don't go in September," Mrs. Milholland fought back whenever she saw
him.

And one day while ironing a shirt, he suddenly looked
through his open door, up into the untroubled blue sky,
and he decided. Simpson was a white man's college,
with white teachers, and he might well be exposing himself to a second spiritual wound. But he had made up his
mind to try.

He worked day and night, seeking out odd jobs when
his scrubbing and ironing were finished. By the end of
August he had repaid all his debts and, in another week,
had put by a small sum to see him through the first days
at Simpson. And before dawn on September 9, 1890, he
set out on the road to Indianola. It was a long walk, almost 30 miles, but even before the sun rose it seemed to
George Carver that there was a light in the sky. Maybe
it was his star. And needing to find out, he walked on,
eagerly, expectantly.

IV. To Learn and Labor Truly

> GEORGE CARVER OFTEN TOOK ME WITH
> HIM ON BOTANY EXPEDITIONS, AND IT
> WAS HE WHO FIRST INTRODUCED ME TO
> THE MYSTERIES OF PLANT FERTILIZATION.
> . . . THIS SCIENTIST, WHO BELONGED TO
> ANOTHER RACE, HAD DEEPENED MY AP-
> PRECIATION OF PLANTS IN A WAY THAT
> I COULD NEVER FORGET.
>
> —Henry A. Wallace,
> Secretary of Agriculture, 1933–1940

A TEACHER WROTE, "He came to Indianola with a satchel full of poverty and a burning zeal to know everything."

He came, also, with an unbidden memory. It rose unexpectedly and swam before his eyes when he saw the pleasant little town, so like Highland with its arches of reddening leaves shading the streets. It dried in his mouth and set drums beating in his heart when he stood in the eerily-familiar shadows of the president's office and said, "My name is George Carver, sir."

The Reverend Edmund M. Holmes regarded the applicant. He, too, saw the dark skin, and perhaps beneath the momentary veneer of apprehension, sensed a core of dignity, determination. Neither mattered. The records that George Carver had put down on the desk

63

showed that he was qualified for admission, and Dr. Holmes reached out to shake his hand. "Welcome to Simpson," he said, and so George became only the second Negro student in the college's history.

"Thank you." The words were pitifully inadequate, of course, but were there *any* words that could properly describe his feelings at this moment?

Dr. Holmes asked him to sit down, and they talked for a while about his contemplated courses of study. Then George said that he would need work and a place to stay. "If there is somewhere I can set up a laundry . . ."

There was an unused shack just off the campus, Dr. Holmes told him, and he was welcome to it. The president promised to notify the student body that they could now bring soiled linens to Mr. Carver.

George came out into brilliant afternoon sunshine that precisely matched the sunshine in his soul. All at once the weariness of his eight-hour walk was gone and, finding his shack, he fell to cleaning it and putting his things away with zest and ardor. Then he went to see the bursar and paid the $12 tuition, reducing his scanty capital to a grand total of ten cents. Still buoyant, nonetheless, he strode north to the square to do some shopping. He made a credit arrangement for the purchase of laundry equipment—tubs, washboard, flatirons, soap, starch—producing his tuition receipt to establish that he was, indeed, enrolled at Simpson. With the very last of his hard cash, he bought some beef suet and corn meal. For now—and in crisis—these could keep him going.

Crisis was soon upon him. With generous intent but a traditionally professional memory, Dr. Holmes had forgotten to announce the opening of the new laundry, and day after day George waited in vain for customers. Afterwards, in a letter to the Milhollands, he would write of this period: "For quite some time I lived on prayer, beef suet and corn meal, being, at the last without the suet and meal."

Meanwhile another calamity threatened. He had registered for classes in etymology, grammar, composition and mathematics, then raced expectantly up the winding stairs to the top floor of the main building and presented himself to Miss Budd, the art teacher.

"I am afraid you don't have the requirements to enroll for art," she said at once. She pretended to busy herself at the desk, but had already noted the frayed jacket and thin wrists of the young man who stood before her awkwardly shifting his feet.

George was staggered. "But drawing is what I do best," he said frantically. "Couldn't I—try?" The heady smell of oil paints and turpentine and charcoal dust were all around him, and the full brightness of day poured down through the skylight so that every canvas stood stark and waiting. And it seemed incredible to him that having tried so hard and journeyed so far he was to be denied this ultimate sanctuary.

Etta M. Budd was herself only a recent graduate of Simpson, a small, perceptive girl whose instincts would sometimes, as now, deny the reality before her eyes: here was a student who plainly would be far better off concentrating on a field of study at which he could earn a livelihood. And knowing this full well, still, something made her say, "Very well, I will let you try. I will tell you at the end of two weeks whether there is any use in your continuing."

Sobered and a little frightened, George went through

the next days with dark questions nagging at his brain: suppose he really had no talent for art? suppose he had been deluding himself all these years? All at once nothing was so important—not any of his other classes, nor all of them together—as this two-week testing time. It came over him with a sense of sudden discovery, shock, that it was his craving to paint, more than anything, that had brought him here. He, George Carver, wanted to become an artist!

One gray day dragged into another. Fellow students regarded him at first with casual curiosity, then ignored him altogether. It seemed to George that all 300 of them regularly hailed one another over his shoulder as they crossed the campus, and huddled in clusters of cameraderie before and after classes. He felt conspicuously alone by day and on the verge of surrender through each restless night. He was positive that his sketches for Miss Budd must be pathetically inadequate—why did she say nothing about them?—and as his slender food supply vanished and still not a single customer appeared, total ruin loomed and pressed down.

He could not wait the whole two weeks. Better to know his fate at once, he decided impulsively one afternoon, and lingered behind after the art class to say clumsily, "Miss Budd, you told me—I mean, there was some question about, about . . ."

"About whether you might continue in the art class?"

"Yes, ma'am."

"I think you may. Please pay the fee for your supplies to the bursar this afternoon."

George's spirits which, for a fleeting instant, had soared, came crashing down in fresh agony. "The fee?" he said bleakly.

"What's the matter, George?" Miss Budd asked.

And all in a rush he told her—how he had counted on his laundry to pay for his needs, how he had set up shop in the deserted shack, and how his tubs had sat empty all these ten days. "So I can't pay the fee this afternoon," he finished sadly. "I don't know when I can pay it."

"I see." Miss Budd tapped her finger, musing, then said, "Well, perhaps the fee can wait a while. I'm certain you'll be earning some money before long."

She was certain, it turned out, because single-handedly she saw to it. First off she announced to her other classes the location of George Carver's excellent laundry service, emphasizing that it awaited their patronage. Then, calling on her friends in the town, she told them that she had a student of real promise who deserved their help: he could do odd jobs of any kind, she said, and needed some warm winter clothing and whatever odds and ends of furniture they might spare.

Returning from classes one afternoon not many days later, George opened his door—and stopped dead in astonishment. For a panicky moment he thought he had blundered into the wrong shanty. In the place of his improvised furnishings—a crate and some stacked boxes —stood a table and two sturdy chairs. The blanket he had left rolled in a corner was now spread neatly on a proper mattress and bedstead. There were dishes on the table, a worn but serviceable overcoat hanging next to his work clothes and, in the kitchen corner, a loaf of freshly-baked bread and a package of stewing meat.

Finally, intuitively, he understood the origin of his windfall. Tears of the most profound gladness sprang to his eyes and, for a while, he wandered aimlessly around the room, just touching his new things—the table, the coat—so deeply stirred by these marks of anonymous goodwill that a sudden knocking at his door brought him up short. He stood stunned, still held silent by emotion until, at last, his first customer shouted, "Hey, anybody home?"

And so George was in business. The crisis was past. Laundry piled up in his lean-to and he boiled and scrubbed it clean by candlelight and before daybreak. And he was never happier. When he tried to thank Miss Budd for all she had done, she made little of it. Instead, she berated him for not wearing the overcoat.

Shyly George said, "Well, it's not very cold out yet and I—I don't want to wear it out."

"Nonsense!" the teacher snapped. "You'll catch your death of cold and then what good will all your laundry work and fine furniture do you? You march right home and get that coat."

And George said, "Yes, ma'am," and did.

All that winter, in an effort to repay Miss Budd's kindness, he found an hour or so each week to cut her firewood and to keep a neat stack piled by her hearth. Learning that a particular friend of hers, Mrs. Arthur Liston, had organized the furniture hunt and delivery to his shanty, he determined that she, too, must have some tangible evidence of his gratitude. Not until the following spring, though, did he find the way to express it. Mrs. Liston, it seems, was a devoted gardener and, with his inimitable touch, George rejuvenated her flower beds and brightened one whole corner with a cluster of amaryllis bulbs. When he painted a picture of the garden in first bloom and presented it to Mrs. Liston, the good lady was overcome.

"It's beautiful," she murmured, holding the picture, gazing at it. "It's just—beautiful. I don't know how to thank you."

"It's the other way around, ma'am," George said. "I'm thanking you—or trying to—for your goodness to me last fall."

It was a significant truth. All his life George Carver would deem it urgent to return kindness for kindness. He wanted unrequited favors no more than he wanted harshness or indifference. If he was to be one with his fellowmen, if he was to be granted what was rightfully his and assume his full share of responsibility, how could he remain in anyone's debt?

Slowly he made friends. As they had in Minneapolis, students who came to leave their laundry stayed to talk with the thin young man whose personal history was so vastly different from their own. Sometimes they just sat listening as he read aloud from a book propped beside the steaming tubs, scrubbing, reading, then scrubbing some more. Sometimes they shared his savory biscuits and honey. And always there were questions: "Well, how did you *live* all that time you were looking for schools?" And, "Where will you go from here, George?"

He had no answer for that last yet. He was happiest painting and sometimes permitted himself flights of fancy in which he saw himself continuing his art studies in Paris, nourishing his yearning to give shape and color to his visions, creating on canvas that world of order and beauty he had so long sought. Meanwhile, though, he was content. The struggle to survive seemed won. Fulfillment now depended on his own skills and energy, and no man, black or white, could ask for more.

"It was in high school that I first learned what it

meant to be a human being," he would say, "and at Simpson that I could truly believe I was one."

Of course he let nothing interfere with his early morning expeditions through the woods. He carried a tin box and into it went stones and slips of unusual plants, and soon every flat surface in his room was crowded with the inexhaustible phenomena of nature. With Miss Budd's encouragement he brought herbs and flowers to the art studio and they grew luxuriantly in the full sunlight. He had progressed from landscapes to still life and his portraits of a rose, a clutch of daisies, were endowed with the loveliness and the life-glow that George saw in every growing thing.

Once, as an exercise, he painted a picture of a cactus grafting experiment that he had devised, and though Miss Budd seemed much taken with it, she didn't return it for a long time. When she did, it was with the plainspoken question that was to orient George Carver's life: "What are your plans for the future?"

He shrugged uneasily. He sensed that something about this picture had brought him to a turning point and he felt unready. "To paint," he answered, "to be an artist—if you think I'm good enough."

"Oh, you're good enough. You have great talent, George. But so few artists can earn a living and you're . . ."

She stopped abruptly and George finished the sentence: ". . . a colored man."

"It's best to face up to facts."

Then there was a burdened silence between them. The darkening art room seemed to George to turn suddenly unsubstantial, unreal. "I have always been able to support myself," he said.

"But do you want always to be washing other people's laundry? Cutting their firewood?" She bent toward him and said, "George, I showed your picture to my father. He's a professor of horticulture at the Iowa Agricultural College at Ames. I told him about your skill with plants. George, he believes you could have a useful, rewarding life in agriculture. He thinks you should be at Ames."

"And you?"

She returned his look and the answer was in her eyes. "I think so, too," Miss Budd said.

Like a millstone, he carried the inexorable need to decide wherever he went. If Miss Budd had never spoken he could have gone on basking in Simpson's warmth— he had his painting, his friends. But once the words were out, the specter of tomorrow haunted him. He was past thirty. He could not forever remain a student.

But why couldn't he become an artist? If he never sold a picture, if he had to live in a shanty all his life and scrub clothes to pay for his meals, it wouldn't matter. It was what he wanted to do with all his heart. And then late one spring night, as he sat on his doorstep and watched the mysterious stars—so many stars, so many paths—the image of Aunt Mariah Watkins sprang suddenly before his mind's eye, and her voice was in his ear. "Be like Libby," she was saying. "Go out in the world and give your learning back to our people. They're starving for a little learning."

And George knew he would go to Ames.

The decade before 1900 was a time of flux and promise for the centuries-old agricultural craft. It was about to become a science. There were men questioning the

rudimentary and time-worn techniques of the family
farm, seeking counteragents against the ravages of nature, new nourishment for land exhausted by uncounted
generations of one-crop harvests. And nowhere were
these revolutionary studies more intensively pursued than
at the Iowa State College of Agriculture and Mechanic
Arts, 50 miles due north of Indianola.

New crops were being tested across its hundreds of
rolling acres. In the laboratories, the magic of chemistry
was brought to bear on the eternal problems of soil
and growth. Uninhibited by the strictures of the past,
undaunted by all the things that farmers said couldn't
be done, the remarkable group of young scientists
gathered at Ames was to regenerate American agriculture, and dominate agricultural thinking for the next
half-century.

Dr. Louis H. Pammell was perhaps the country's pre-
eminent botanist. James G. Wilson, Dean of Agriculture
and director of the experimental station, was to become
President McKinley's Secretary of Agriculture in six
years, and stay on through the administrations of Theodore Roosevelt and William H. Taft. His assistant,
Professor Henry Cantwell Wallace, would distinctively
fill that same post for Presidents Coolidge and Harding.
And just learning to walk when George Carver came to
Ames in May, 1891, was "Uncle Henry's" boy, young
Henry Wallace, who in 1932 was to be named Secretary
of Agriculture by Franklin D. Roosevelt and, eight years
later, to be elected Vice President of the United States.

George was properly inspired by the green campus
and buildings—it was by far the largest school he had
ever seen. But he'd arrived at an inauspicious time. The
college year followed the planting season, February to

November, and in May, with the semester well begun, no one seemed to know of an available room for the new student. "Tama Jim," as Professor Wilson was called by the undergraduates, a hearty and warm-natured man, roared like a bull when this unhappy word reached his office.

"Send him to me!" he bellowed. "*I* have a room for him!"

Whereupon he swept his papers off the desk and moved up to the second floor. He then ordered a cot and chest brought to his old office and this, the most spacious room in North Hall, became the quarters of the astonished and thankful newcomer.

But there remained still another trial ahead for George —as, indeed, there would always be another trial ahead —and he met this one with the same dignity and quiet grace with which he was to face all the large and little affronts flung at him because his skin was dark. He could not eat in the dining hall, someone told him. He would have to take his meals in the basement with the kitchen help and field hands. This he did without objection; hurt, yes, and cast down at being shut away from student talk and friendship, but reasoning that if the whites upstairs weren't really better than he was, neither was he any better than the hired help who had to eat in the basement.

And so matters might have rested had not Professor Budd, writing to his daughter in Indianola, mentioned George's banishment from the dining hall. While Miss Budd could not leave at mid-semester, Mrs. Liston could—and did! Clapping a hat on her head, she took the next train to Ames, descended on a startled and slightly suspicious George, and spent the day being dutifully impressed as he showed her around the campus and introduced her to his teachers. Sure enough, at dinnertime, Mrs. Liston insisted that she meant to eat in the basement with her friend.

"But—but, madame," the nervous and suddenly miserable dining hall director pleaded, "what will the Dean say? And Professor Wilson . . ."

"You ought to have considered that when you arranged Mr. Carver's dining facilities," the indignant lady snapped back, and threw over her shoulder as she started down the stairs, "And please bear in mind that I expect to be visiting here again."

George introduced Mrs. Liston to his friends in the basement and they all enjoyed a lively mealtime conversation. But when he came to breakfast next morning, he was asked if he would be kind enough to join the other students: there was a place for him at table six.

He was a favorite from the first, his extra years and a wide-ranging knowledge commanding respect, and his enthusiasm for undergraduate antics effectively undermining attempts to cloak him in aloofness. Within a week he had devised a table game that swept the dining hall and remains an institution at Ames to this day. Each dish and condiment had to be asked for by its scientific name. "Please pass the salt," would produce a howl of pitying laughter—but no salt. If you remembered *Triticum vulgare*, you could fill up on bread, but would find the potatoes forever out of reach should the magic words, *solanum tuberosum*, elude you—unless you were lucky enough to be seated next to George Carver. Inventor and now the arbiter of the game, still he couldn't resist a plea for help. "What's the formula for sugar, George?" a boy would meekly whisper after poking at his tasteless oatmeal. And George would whisper back, "C twelve, H twenty-two, O eleven," and look around guiltily to see if he'd been caught.

His course of studies was imposing. Ever conscious of the fleeting years, he enrolled for botany, geometry, chemistry, zoology, bacteriology and entomology. He sometimes awed his teachers, not only with his remarkable fund of information, but with an intuitive grasp of the most subtle theory. Chemistry, especially, intrigued him. To break down a familiar substance to its component parts, to get to the mysterious heart of things— this, at last, was a beginning answer to his whys and how-comes.

Geometry was an exception, a chink in his scholastic armor. There was something about lines and angles that eluded him—*why* was triangle one congruent to triangle two, and what if it was?—and he barely stumbled by. Writing to the Milhollands, he said of Professor Stanton, his geometry teacher, "Stanty, as he is affectionately known, does all within his power to enthuse and inspire me in the science of plane geometry, but having such poor material to work with, his efforts are not crowned with very brilliant success."

Though he worked, as always, to support himself—as a janitor in North Hall, waiter, greenhouse and laboratory caretaker—he found time for a full program of extracurricular activity. He was invited to join Welch Eclectic, a literary society, and participated fully in readings and debates. His voice was still high-pitched and apt to break altogether in mid-sentence, but George refused to let embarrassment smother his hankering to express himself. And, indeed, though his audience might snap to amused attention at the first girlish-sounding utterance from the lanky young man, it was his intense delivery and a sharp sense of drama that ultimately held them. Doggedly he practiced speaking and singing, and won a place with a college quartet. One evening, after a songfest at an entertainment in town, he was approached by a faculty member of the Boston Conservatory of Music, prepared to offer him a scholarship on the spot. George declined—if painting as a life's work smacked of self-indulgence, so did a career in music. But he always regarded that as the moment when he finally triumphed over his capricious voice.

Somehow he became the official trainer for the athletic teams and before long knew as much about the human anatomy as any physician. But even in the beginning, as a raw "rubber," there seemed to be magic in his slender fingers. He could massage the bone-weariness out of an exhausted football player, knead the cramps from the legs of a trackman. "Doctor," was the caption for his picture in *Bomb*, the usually teasing college annual, "whom not even the critics criticize."

Since Iowa Agriculture was supported by the state, male students were required to join the National Guard Student battalion on campus, to drill in navy blue cadet uniforms and attend lectures on military tactics. George, of course, knew that he could never become an army officer—Negroes simply didn't. Nevertheless—and perhaps in a kind of eloquent protest—he applied himself assiduously to the program. When General James Rush Lincoln, the brusque and fire-breathing commander of the Ames contingent, upbraided him for his chronic slouch, he determined that somehow he would overcome this heritage of all his years of stooping over laundry tubs. And he did, walking two miles or more each

morning with his hands clasped behind his back and a
sturdy stick wedged under his armpits. Not even when
he spotted a tempting botanical specimen did he bend
—he dropped to his knees for a closer examination. The
results were soon apparent and in two years George
went from cadet to captain, the top student rating.
There is a photograph of him standing stern and ramrod
straight in his uniform, but the real mark of his success
was General Lincoln's tribute: "This most gentlemanly
and efficient cadet," said the officer whose very glance
could set the entire corps quivering, "has risen to the
rank of captain through personal determination and
merit alone, and I couldn't be prouder of him."

For nearly a year George had not touched a paint-
brush. His oils and canvases were locked away in a case,
a part of his life shut up as though in fear that the very
sight of them would seduce him away from his private
pledge to serve others. Now, though, his resolve strengthened by real progress toward a real goal, he poked
tentatively into the locked case, made some sketches,
even set up his easel. Soon he was painting signs and
pictures with which to decorate the Eclectic Society
meeting room. When winter vacation arrived, he rushed
back to Simpson to enroll in Miss Budd's art class.

She was delighted to see him, of course, but there was
little more she could teach him. "He had an instinctive
feeling for form," she has said, "and though I could
make an occasional suggestion about color, I no longer
dared intrude myself on his genius." And so George
spent the days painting the yucca plant he remembered
so vividly from his desert wanderings, a vase of roses,
peonies. He lost himself in the miracle of creativity, one
with his brushes and at peace with all the world. It was

during this winter of 1891–1892 that he made some of his most memorable paintings.

Back at Ames in February, he plunged again into a hectic pace of study and work, fully intending to return to Simpson the following winter. But his grinding schedule took its toll. In the fall he fell ill with anemia, and so overwhelming was his commitment to himself, so distraught was he over missing his classes and added obligations, that he flayed his nerves to the very edge of a breakdown. Under no circumstances was he to leave the campus, the college doctor ordered, and so it was.

He was short of money, too. One day, with snow heavy on the ground, Professor Wilson noted the deplorable condition of his shoes. At once he pulled some money from his billfold and thrust it into George's fist. "I want you to go and buy yourself a new pair of shoes," he said. And before George could so much as frame a protest, he roared, "At once!" And George fled.

The Iowa State Teachers Association was meeting in Cedar Rapids between Christmas and New Year's, with an all-Iowa art exhibit to be an important part of the program. Did George plan to show any of his paintings? Professor Budd asked.

"I'm afraid I can't afford the trip," was the straightforward reply.

"Ah, that's too bad," said the teacher thoughtfully. "My daughter tells me that in her opinion you are the best painter in Iowa."

"She's most kind," George said, smiling, "and perhaps a little prejudiced." And he went about his business, trying very hard to put down a useless longing to go to Cedar Rapids.

The day after Christmas he sat in his room and

watched a fresh-falling snow. A wreath in his window
marked the holiday season, but George wore his patched
and tattered work clothes: he was to earn some money
that afternoon by restoring order to a faculty member's
house after the Christmas festivities. Soon the sleigh
Dr. Brady had sent for him pulled up outside North
Hall and George threw on his hand-me-down overcoat
and ran out.

Dr. Brady, however, was not at the reins. A student
was, and heavily-bundled students sat, sprawled and
dangled all over the sleigh. "Well, I thought . . ."
George began doubtfully.

"Climb aboard!" the driver yelled to him. "We'll take
you where you want to go."

Somehow they made room for him, but it was soon
clear that the sleigh was bypassing faculty row and
bound for town. Furthermore, other boys, in groups of
two and three, had suddenly materialized on the road
and were trotting alongside.

"Say, what is this all about?" George said, squirm-
ing.

"It's all about Christmas!" someone cried irrelevantly,
and the others yowled in merry agreement.

"Well, you'd better let me off!" George shouted. "I'm
supposed . . ."

"Sit down!" they commanded, and, "We know what
you're supposed to do!" Then they burst into chorus
after rousing chorus of *Jingle Bells,* ignoring George and
his protests, except to pull him back down whenever
the sleigh slowed enough for him to have a try at scrambling out.

Presently they stopped in front of a men's clothing
store. "Let's go, George!" they sang out.

"But I can't go in there! I'm wearing these old working clothes."

"That's just what we came to see about!" And they all but carried him inside.

The salesman, who seemed quite prepared for this headlong invasion by the cheery, jumbling mob, promptly produced a handsome gray suit. "If you'll just try this for size," he said.

Thrust forward by his captors, George scolded, "This fooling has gone far enough. I'm not buying any clothes."

But the fact was that he had not much choice. Struggling, he was jostled into a dressing room, swiftly divested of his own trousers and buttoned into the gray suit, which the boys solemnly adjudged a proper fit. Whereupon they whisked the reluctant model, by now speechless and utterly bewildered, back out front and ordered a hat, shirt, tie, gloves, shoes and socks. Finally he was helped into a new black overcoat and, as chaotically as they had burst in, the whole band stormed out, George in their midst, to be wedged down in the sleigh again, his boggling questions drowned in still another wave of *Jingle Bells*.

"Well, then, who's going to pay for all this?" he shouted once into the relative quiet between bars. But the only answer he got was:

"Oh what fun it is to ride
In a one-horse o-open sleigh!"

They stopped and George barely had time to realize they were in front of the Wilson house before he had been whisked inside. There, grinning in the parlor, stood Professors Wilson and Budd, and for the first time since he'd been swept up by the pandemonium in front of North Hall, George gained someone's full attention. "Sir," he said carefully to Professor Wilson, "I am supposed to be working this afternoon."

"Indeed."

"Yes. I promised to clean Dr. Brady's house. But these men . . ."

"You are going to Cedar Rapids this afternoon."

"Hear, hear!" someone called out.

". . . brought me here," George finished with an awed, barely audible whisper.

"George," Professor Wilson said into the room's sudden hush, "many of us here are determined that Iowa Agriculture shall be properly represented at the Teachers Association art exhibit. Here is your ticket to Cedar Rapids and here are the paintings Professor Budd spirited from your quarters—with his daughter's counsel."

Numbly, automatically, George took the envelope. He touched the heavily-wrapped canvases. "But Dr. Brady . . ." he said.

"A suitable arrangement has been made with Dr. Brady. He is delighted that you are going."

"But the money—all the money. How will I ever repay it?" He was truly concerned. He wanted no one's charity.

"You have already repaid it." Professor Wilson clamped a massive hand on George's frail shoulder and said, "My boy, the small sum each of your classmates and teachers contributed is little enough for the honor of your friendship. We believe in you." He cleared his throat. "Besides, it is too late for you to do anything but go. Your work is already listed in the catalogue."

George blinked several times, his eyes misting, and

holding the little booklet, read, "G.W. Carver, No. 25: *Roses;* No. 43: *Peonies;* No. 99: *Yucca gloriosa;* No. 186: *Vase of Flowers.*"

He looked from one to another of them, failing altogether in his first attempt to speak. Finally he murmured, "I thank you. I—thank all of you." Then he turned away, for he was crying quite freely.

Iowa Agriculture's faith was not misplaced. At the exhibit—which, on arrival in Cedar Rapids, George characteristically volunteered to help set up—all four of his pictures were awarded prizes, and *Yucca gloriosa* was chosen to be shown the following summer at the World's Columbian Exposition in Chicago. There, in competition with the work of professionals from all over the world, it won honorable mention, and newspapers across Iowa took note of George Carver's triumph. But not the prizes and not the sudden spurt of fame moved him nearly so much as that moment of comradeship in Professor Wilson's parlor.

George graduated in 1894, the precious and long-sought Bachelor of Science degree won with a thesis entitled *Plants As Modified By Man.* He was near the top of his class and Dr. Pammell placed him among the most brilliant students he had ever taught. A florist in Ames offered him a job, but he turned it down, though he did not yet know how he would earn a livelihood. "I didn't struggle for my education in order to arrange flowers for the dead," he said.

Mrs. Liston came on from Indianola to be on hand for the graduation exercises. She brought a bouquet of red carnations, a gift from Miss Budd and George's former classmates at Simpson. Much moved, he put one of the blooms in his lapel and, to the best of anyone's knowledge, wore a flower, a sprig of evergreen, even a weed—some small growing thing—every day of his life thereafter. It was to Mrs. Liston that he confided a tremulant hope. There was an opening for an assistant botanist in the experiment station and he had applied for the job.

"But I am not counting that particular chicken," he said with a wry smile. "There are many qualified applicants and, after all, there has never been a colored man on the faculty before."

"Neither has a colored man ever graduated from this college before," said Mrs. Liston briskly. "I think you will get it."

A few days later Dr. Pammell sent for him. "Well, sir, what are your plans?" he asked.

George's heart shrivelled at what he took to be a polite dismissal. "I hadn't thought," he mumbled. "I mean, perhaps some small school would take me."

"Take you? You're already taken!" Pammell suddenly smiled broadly, his teeth flashing in a black beard. "You are my new assistant and I want to know what plans you have for the experiment station. Would you like to take over the greenhouse?"

George had stopped breathing. Now, as though it were someone else, he heard the air rush from his lungs. Dr. Pammell's words tumbled in his brain, settled themselves at last—*Would you like to take over the greenhouse?*—and he replied buoyantly, "I would indeed, sir! And—I'm deeply grateful."

"We're grateful to have you, Carver. There isn't a better man for the job anywhere."

It was demanding work, but George felt rewarded

every time he set foot in the greenhouse. Once he hauled sacks of potting earth there, and swept broken pottery from the floor. Now he was in charge, a chore boy no more. He was—and he had to repeat it to himself again and again to believe it—a scientist.

The campus was astir with portents of things to come. Around Professor Wallace there clustered a band of young intellectuals whose energies were channeled into the search for a strain of corn that would withstand assaults of disease and drought. Pammell's published studies on plant pathology—on two of which his new assistant collaborated—were to become landmarks in their field. Agriculture was freshly viewed as the great mother science—"Nations last only as long as their topsoil lasts," said Wallace—and the complex trinity of relationship between earth, plant and man was scrutinized as never before.

George cast himself wholeheartedly into this questing atmosphere. He was studying for his master's degree while working as station assistant, concentrating especially on mycology, that branch of botany dealing with fungus growths. Soon his collection consisted of some 20,000 specimens and his skill at hybridizing rendered whole families of fruits and plants resistant to fungus attack. Scientific papers began to cite G.W. Carver as their authority. He crossed and recrossed the Iowa countryside lecturing on horticulture and mycology, using strikingly graphic examples to impress basic truths on his audiences of farmers and county agents: "If you took an Iowan to the North Pole and left him there, it would be necessary to provide him with food and warm clothing or he would perish. In the same way, you cannot plant an apple tree in alien ground and expect it to

flourish without special care." The boy plant doctor of
Diamond Grove was now ministering to the needs of
all the agricultural community.

Mornings found him tramping the mud sloughs and
rushes along the Skunk River, ever ready to drop to his
knees for an eye-to-leaf inspection of ailing growth.
Had it been weakened by a fungus? And was it a type
he hadn't seen before? Often his shoes squished and his
trousers were soaked from the thighs down, but he
seemed heedless of any discomfort as he peered at a
slip of browning vegetation and pondered its mycological significance.

On one such outing, not far from the campus, he was
approached by a tow-headed boy of six who, in the
straightforward way of small boys, asked what he was
doing.

"I'm looking for a fungus," George said, not taking
his eyes from the water lily over which he was bent.

"What's a fungus?"

George straightened up. The boy gazed at him earnestly, solemnly, and waited for an answer. "Well,"
George said slowly, "a fungus is a growing thing that
lives on other growing things, like a mushroom or a
toadstool. Have you ever seen a toadstool?"

"Uh huh."

"Good. Now here's another kind of fungus." He
showed the boy a scattering of dark mold on the lily.
"It eats into the plant and makes it sick."

"Are you going to make it better?"

George smiled. "I'm going to try." He got to his feet
and the two started back toward the college, the tall
scientist and the serious gray-eyed little boy. "Where
do you live?" George asked as they walked along.

"Up there on the hill. In the yellow house."

"Professor Wallace's house?"

"Uh huh. I'm young Henry."

And so began a friendship that was to last half a century, firmly rooted in affection and mutual regard. Hand in hand and day after day the two would hike across marshes and upland, the boy keenly responsive as George directed his attention beyond nature's outer guise to reveal the secrets of the earth. Grasses, which looked identical, were in fact as different as people, and young Henry quickly learned to recognize the minute blossoms which characterized the separate species. He gained from the assistant botanist a lasting affection for the amaryllis, and years later they were still exchanging unusual specimens.

In the greenhouse, George showed the eager youngster how he crossed plants, taking the stamen from one and putting it carefully on the pistils of another. Engrossed, the boy watched George graft a red rose on a yellow rose bush, slitting the bark and splicing in a tiny cutting.

"But what's the *good* of grafting?" Henry wanted to know, and George remembered with sudden poignance his own little boy's need to understand *why* the roses by the Carver cabin door were yellow and those by the window red.

"For many reasons," he said, speaking as though to another adult. "Grafting can speed up growing time. Or a plant that cannot survive in this climate may do very well if its root is grafted onto the root of a more hardy plant."

Soon young Henry was having a try at crossing and grafting himself. He studied seed pollen under microscope. And long afterward Vice-President Henry A. Wallace was to write of this motivating time in his life: "Though I was a small boy, I am certain now that, out of the goodness of his heart, Dr. Carver greatly exaggerated my botanical ability. But his faith aroused my natural interest and kindled an ambition to excel in this field; his praise did me good, as praise of a child often does."

George remained a best friend through all the boy's growing-up years, and a mark of that friendship was that people would come to say of the lastingly-inspirited young Henry that he could grow corn on a wood floor, and today the Wallace-developed hybrid stands tall and straight in the wind across vast stretches of the Midwest. They were never long out of touch and corresponded until George Carver died, exchanging ideas and thrashing out all manner of agricultural and human problems.

In 1896 George received his master's degree in agriculture and bacterial botany. He had never been more content—and was sometimes vaguely disturbed by his happiness. Was his work in Iowa really a fulfillment of his obligation? He was a Negro, and across the land millions of his people, starved and stultified, yearned for a place in the sun. Did he serve them best as an example of what a man—any man—could achieve by unending effort? Or did he belong among them, sharing with them the knowledge he had come by with such labor and pain? Alone in the woods, or under the limitless night sky, he thought of Libby, the slave woman of Aunt Mariah's girlhood, who, at the risk of banishment, had taught other slaves to read; and of Aunt Mariah herself,

who had sheltered him and sent him out into the world
to "give your learning back to our people."

God, of course, had a plan for him and, in His own
good time, God would tell him what he must do. Meanwhile, questions nagged at his brain and something,
some mysterious new path, seemed to lie just beyond his
vision.

It was about this same time, in an Alabama town 800
miles away, that a man named Booker T. Washington
struggled to keep alive the flickering dream of a colored
people's institute of learning. He had little to work with,
and less money. But he did have a fiery sense of mission, an absolute determination that if human will and
toil, no matter how menial, could raise the colored people from the depths of their ignorance and poverty, then
they would be raised. He was the acknowledged spokesman of all the Negro race, yet had to face and fight off
disaster with every new day.

"These people do not know how to plow or plant or
harvest," he wrote. "I am not skilled at such things. I
teach them how to read, to write, to make good shoes,
good bricks, and how to build a wall. I cannot give
them food and so they starve."

He kept comparing the pathetic handful of souls at
his school with the multitudes he could not hope to
reach, and he became resolved that his most urgent
need was someone who *could* teach his people to plant
and harvest. Somewhere, he had heard that there was a
noted agriculturist, a colored man, at a school in Iowa,
and on April 1, 1896, Washington sat down to write
him a letter:

"I cannot offer you money, position, or fame. The first
two you have. The last, from the place you now occupy,

you will no doubt achieve. These things I now ask you to give up. I offer you in their place work—hard, hard work—the task of bringing a people from degradation, poverty and waste to full manhood."

And on a morning four days later, a tall, hawk-faced young man stood reading the letter in the pale sunshine of early spring, the rich Iowa countryside greening with promise on every side. And his blood raced and his heart beat fast: God had revealed His plan for George Carver.

V. Tuskegee

> YOUR DEPARTMENT EXISTS ONLY ON
> PAPER, CARVER, AND YOUR LABORATORY
> WILL HAVE TO BE IN YOUR HEAD.
>
> —*Booker T. Washington*

Booker TALIAFERRO WASHINGTON was born into slavery, most likely in 1856, on the Burroughs plantation in Franklin County, Virginia. His mother was a cook in the "big house" and each Sunday was permitted to bring some molasses home to her three children. Home was a fourteen-by-sixteen cabin in the slave quarter, with earthen floor and no windows. For Booker, raised on an unvarying ration of corn bread and fat pork, that bit of molasses was a heart-stopping treat.

Sometimes he was called up to the mansion to shoo flies from the dining room table, and even as a boy was highly valued: court records show that his worth was assessed at $400. Of his father he knew only that he was a white man from some neighboring plantation. He was not yet ten when the Civil War ended and the slaves were freed. He remembers an army officer standing on the veranda of the colonnaded white house and reading to the assembled Negroes what must have been the Emancipation Proclamation. "You are free," the man said, and Booker felt his mother's tears as she stooped to kiss him, and there was tumult and song and great shouts of rejoicing that lasted into the night.

Then, like a soft cloud turned abruptly dark and ominous, sober second thoughts overtook the people. They turned to each other with plaintive questions—how were they to live? where would their food come from now, and clothing and shelter? who would take care of the old folks? where should they go?—and there were no answers.

"It was very much like suddenly turning a youth of ten or twelve years out into the world to provide for himself," Washington later wrote. "In a few hours the great questions with which the Anglo-Saxon race had been grappling for centuries had been thrown upon these people to be solved."

Almost alone among colored leaders, Washington would see that emancipation itself answered no questions, solved no problems. Four million souls had been flung into a strange and alien liberty without money, homes, jobs or votes. They had been declared free—but free for what? To vie with their onetime masters? To compete for livelihood and station with the very white men who attributed the South's ruin to Negro aspirations?

Inevitably there were false starts. The road ahead was a hundred years long and strewn with pitfalls and delusion. And only a few would ever understand that the true beginning must be made at the very bottom of the pit. To them Booker T. Washington devoted his life, struggling always to make meaningful this newfound freedom of body, to put into unskilled black hands the tools of learning and enterprise and opportunity.

His incredible journey from slavery to the Hall of Fame began that year of 1865. Young Booker and his

family crossed the mountains into West Virginia's Ka-
nawha Valley, taking turns riding in a splintery, mule-
drawn cart, but mostly trotting alongside, day after day,
mile after weary mile. In Malden, a tiny town close to
Charleston, the mother's husband, Booker's stepfather,
awaited them, and promptly sent the nine-year-old boy
and his brother to work in the salt furnaces. For seven
years Booker scooped and packed salt and hacked coal
in the mine bottom dark, and inspirited with a hunger to
read and write, scrapped and scrambled his way to a
rudimentary education.

Nearly everything he read and heard told him that
the Negro race was the lowest and most hopeless of
God's creatures. "At first," he was to write, "I wanted to
go away to some distant part of the earth and bury myself where I might be a stranger to all of my people."
But the ultimate effect of this adolescent purgatory was
to drive him closer to them. "I determined to spend my
life proving to the world that it should learn to respect
them, both for what they were and what they should be
able to do."

In 1872, having heard somewhere that there was a
place called Hampton Institute, a school for Negroes,
near Norfolk, he set out to arm himself for his great task,
begging rides and walking the whole 500 miles across
hostile, Reconstruction-torn Virginia. Working as a janitor to pay his way, studying with selfless intensity, he
graduated in 1875 and returned to Malden to teach the
Negro school there. His classes ran from eight in the
morning until ten at night, filled with youngsters by
day and adults at night. And to both groups, along with
the lessons in writing and reading, went lectures on the
importance of the bath, the comb and the toothbrush.

Four years later, Washington went back to Hampton

to take a teaching post. He was there, in May 1881, when General Samuel C. Armstrong, the principal, received an urgent request from a group of people in a place called Tuskegee, deep in the "black belt" of Alabama: the Legislature had authorized a normal school for Negroes; could General Armstrong send a white person to organize and teach such a school at once? The General wrote in reply that he had no white teacher available for such a project, but could recommend a colored man whose qualifications and capacities were eminently suited to the post. His name was Booker T. Washington. Three days later, Sunday, a messenger delivered a telegram to General Armstrong during evening worship services in the chapel. "Booker T. Washington will suit us," it said. "Send him at once."

Tuskegee was a nervous little town of 1000 whites and 1000 Negroes. It had been spared the worst agonies of the war, but the landowners still longed for their graceful and uncomplicated yesterdays, and the sharecroppers cast bitter eyes on their colored competitors, and the politicians contrived to hang on to their offices in a chaotic Reconstruction which had given the black man a vote.

"What can I do for your people in exchange for their support?" W.F. Foster, a former Confederate officer and now an aspirant to the State Legislature, had asked Lewis Adams, who was once a slave.

Adams did not hesitate. He had been acknowledged by his white father and permitted a basic education, to which he now owed his success as a skilled metal worker and his position as leader of Tuskegee's colored population. Learning was to him real and relevant, and he said that if Foster would promise to work in the Legislature for a Negro training school in Tuskegee, "I will bend every effort to secure for you the colored vote."

The bargain was made and Colonel Foster was duly elected to the State Senate where, true to his word, he introduced a bill which appropriated $2000 for staff salaries and authorized the establishment of "a Normal School for colored teachers." There was resistance, re-criminations *—"If you educate the niggers who'll do the work?"—but on February 12, 1881 the bill became law, and the search for someone to teach the teachers began.

Booker Washington came to Tuskegee in June and went to stay with Lewis Adams. His "school" consisted of the Methodist Episcopal church building, a leaky frame structure that threatened momentarily to collapse of its own weight, and a nearby shanty whose condition was worse yet. There were no books, no slates, no desks and no students. One teacher, a white man, recruited before Washington, had taken a horrified look at the physical plant, listened to what was expected of him—and fled.

Washington was no less disillusioned, but would not be balked. There was in him a certain remarkable mettle, a gritty buoyancy, so that in the face of apparently insuperable difficulty, he seemed to grow larger than life, transported by the call to battle. Two days after his arrival, he had borrowed a mule and wagon and set out along the dusty roads to learn what he could about the people and their needs, and to let the people know that a teacher, someone who cared, was among them. For a

* Foster's political career was brief. Goaded by fears of a Negro awakening, the Colonel's white constituents branded him a "nigger-lover" and swept him from office.

month he wandered the countryside, sleeping each night
in a different cabin, listening to the laments of benighted,
poverty-racked farmers, gleaning from them their meager hopes and the hopes they cherished for their children.
He tried valiantly to infuse them with a sense of worth,
but he was fighting a tragic and corrosive history. Of
an old man who told of being sold into slavery years before, he asked, "How many of you were there?"

"Five," was the reply. "Myself and brother and three
mules."

By the time Washington returned to Tuskegee, his
task loomed like a mountain in his path and he felt utterly inadequate to it—and he fell to work. School con-
vened in the dilapidated church on July 4, 1881. There
were 30 pupils, most of them older than the teacher.
When it rained, a scholar held an umbrella over Washington's head and the lesson proceeded, and when
winter came and the wind blew the class huddled low on
the floor to escape the worst blasts. But each morning
Washington went down the line of his students con-
demning muddy shoes, collarless shirts and soiled trousers. "What is the news?" he would ask, and when a
group excitedly told him about a big fist fight, he acidly
remarked that that was no news at all, only gossip, and
for the next day's lesson assigned them the duty of finding out what was happening in the Legislature.

Late that year, Washington heard that 100 acres of
an abandoned plantation about a mile north of town
could be purchased for $500. The land was arid, bare
except for four ruined buildings, and the price was high.
But Washington now had 50 pupils and dreams for 50
times that number, and he wrote to General Armstrong at
Hampton, begging for a loan for which he promised to
assume personal responsibility. The money came by re-

turn mail and, only days later, teacher and students were swarming through the plantation cabin, kitchen, stable and hen house, hammering, scrubbing, whitewashing.

A new teacher, Miss Olivia A. Davidson, who was to become Washington's wife, undertook to raise enough money to pay off the awesome debt. She canvassed the community, organized festivals, concerts and suppers. People offered gifts according to their means. "I have no money," said an old colored lady who hobbled up to Washington one day, "but I want you to take this toward the learning of the young 'uns." And she put six eggs down on the desk. Within five months the entire $500 had been repaid.

Meanwhile land was cleared and a crop planted. To most of the students, swinging an ax and turning ground was a far cry from the "education" they had envisioned. Somehow they had become suffused with the idea that learning would forever free them from toil and hardship, that school was an escape from work. But when Dr. Washington, the principal, strode out among them with an ax on his shoulder, wielding it with vigor and skill, their mutterings died away; it was a graphic lesson in the dignity of labor, the basic precept on which Tuskegee Institute would grow and flourish.

But it was an unending battle. Each group of incoming students would have to be impressed anew with the truth that a man was not demeaned just because he worked with his hands. They had grown up in the grinding poverty that was the net gain of their parents' unending toil and, with childlike faith, believed that school was not only a magic release from manual labor but would somehow equip them to live in easy affluence ever after. They wanted to study banking and commerce, but they still counted with their fingers and most of them still ate with their fingers. So Washington taught them to wash and plow and plant, aiming to turn out, not scholars, but teachers and technicians and competent farmers. He saw Tuskegee as a place from which generations of graduates would set forth to teach "the man farthest down," who would, in turn, pass on his knowledge, until the influence of the school permeated a whole people.

"No race that has anything to contribute to the markets of the world is long in any degree ostracized," he told them, and they listened and, reluctantly, perhaps, as in the morning one reluctantly yields up a cherished dream, they put away their glib notions and went to work.

When 20 acres were cleared and planted, they fell to constructing a three-story frame building which, despite the typical blunders of novice carpenters, was ready for occupancy by late November. Here, in Porter Hall, the students dedicated their chapel on Thanksgiving Day, and here they slept shivering through the winter, for there were not nearly enough blankets to go around. Now there were 150 students and four teachers and still another building, this one of brick, was needed. They dug clay on the edge of the school property, built a kiln that failed, then another and another—Washington pawned his watch for $15 to pay for one final effort—and at last Alabama Hall rose, four stories tall, solid and true. Washington never got around to redeeming his watch, but he went on to make millions of bricks, for school buildings and for all the Tuskegee community.

In the next 15 years, 40 buildings were erected, all but four by student labor, and in each new class the Tuskegee spirit was quick to assert itself. A freshman, blithely carving his initials in a dormitory door had his jackknife snatched from his hand. "I built that door," barked the indignant upperclassman, "and if you put another mark in it I'll knock you down!"

As building and brick-making became Institute courses, so were other departments created out of school needs. Since there was no money to buy wagons, a wheelwright's class was begun. A onetime slave brought his tinsmithy to the campus and showed the students how to make all their own knives and forks. Lewis Adams taught harness-making. John Washington, the principal's brother, launched a course in bee culture, and the dining room was supplied with honey.

"We ask for nothing which we can do for ourselves," Dr. Washington said. "Nothing has been bought that the students could produce."

No one worked harder than the principal. He taught classes and conducted Sunday evening bible classes. He supervised the brick-making and land-clearing, mended fences, checked and ordered supplies, inspected the dormitories and kitchen and seemed instantly available to any student troubled by news from home or by the complexities of this strange new life at school. Tom Campbell, who was Washington's driver in those crucial first years, reports that every second was urgent to him and that delay of any kind infuriated him. "Sometimes, when he came back from a trip and I would be down to the depot to meet him, he would grab the reins and drive himself, and I really felt sorry for the horses." It was as though he were forever pressed by all the things that needed to be done, and forewarned by some dark premonition that his time on earth was limited.

Washington traveled widely in those days, promoting

interest—and funds—for the new school, and addressing himself to a better understanding between the white and colored races. Before long his name and work were known across the country and when Frederick Douglass, the first great spokesman of the Negro people died in 1895, the mantle of leadership passed logically and inevitably to the shoulders of the slave boy who had fought his way up from deepest darkness. That very year, the nation was astonished to learn that he had been invited to speak at the Atlanta Cotton States and International Exposition.

This great trade fair had been conceived as a demonstration to all the world that the onetime Confederacy had come all the way back from the devastation of the Civil War. King Cotton was again ensconced on his throne and ready to do business with Northern merchants and foreign mills. But to permit a Negro on the same platform with Southern leaders, cried the diehards—with President Cleveland himself!—was to confess before the world that blacks and whites were equal after all.

Washington was painfully aware of the stakes. On what he said and how he said it hung the fortunes of his people for years, perhaps decades, to come. He labored long and hard over his speech, read it to the assembled faculty at Tuskegee, who seemed to think well of it, and still felt "as I suppose a man feels when he is on his way to the gallows" as he climbed aboard the train to Atlanta on the morning of September 17.

Thousands of people had elbowed their way into the auditorium, the Negroes in the gallery cheering when Dr. Washington appeared, the whites ominously quiet. James Creelman's dispatch to the New York *World* tells what happened next:

"He turned his wonderful countenance to the sun without a blink of the eyelids and began to talk. There was a remarkable figure, tall, bony, straight as a Sioux Chief, high forehead, straight nose, heavy jaws, and strong, determined manner. His voice rang out clear and true, and he paused impressively as he made each point. Within ten minutes the multitude was in an uproar of enthusiasm —handkerchiefs were waved, canes were flourished, hats were tossed in the air. The fairest women of Georgia stood and cheered. It was as if the orator had bewitched them."

He told them the parable of the ship lost at sea, its crew dying of thirst. Sighting another vessel, the unfortunates hoisted a signal for water, and the answer came back, "Cast down your bucket where you are." Again and again they ran up their plea, and each time the reply was the same: "Cast down your bucket where you are." Finally, desperate, the captain ordered a bucket put down over the side—and it came up filled with sparkling fresh water. The distressed vessel was at rest in the great mouth of the Amazon River.

Brown fist clenched in the air, Booker T. Washington declared, "To those of my race who depend on bettering their condition in a foreign land or who underestimate the importance of cultivating friendly relations with the Southern white man, who is their next-door neighbor, I would say: 'Cast down your bucket where you are.' To those of the white race, I would repeat what I say to my own race, 'Cast down your bucket where you are.' Cast it down among the eight million Negroes whose habits you know, whose fidelity and love you have tested. Cast down your bucket among these people who have tilled your fields, cleared your forests, builded your railroads and cities."

The audience roared its approval, but were quickly

silent when the speaker raised his open hand. And then Washington uttered the single sentence that brought his listeners to their feet in a fresh storm of applause—and would call down on his head the calumny of a new generation of Negro leaders:

"In all things that are purely social we can be as separate as the fingers"—here he dramatically closed his fist again—"yet one as the hand in all things essential to mutual progress."

Incredibly, Washington's five-minute speech turned out to be the climactic high point of the entire Exposition. Newspapers across the nation printed it verbatim. The Atlanta *Constitution* reported that "That man's speech is the beginning of a moral revolution in America." And President Cleveland wrote, "The Exposition would be fully justified if it did not do more than furnish an opportunity for its delivery." Overnight Booker T. Washington had become one of the most famous men in the land, and the problems and yearnings of his people were understood as never before.

But the scathing counter-reaction was not long in following. To many of his own race, Washington's seeming willingness to surrender Negro social and political claims was nothing short of outright betrayal. "Uncle Tom!" they jeered at him, and insisted that the Negro's strong right arm would gain for him every prerogative to which he was entitled, and that, if it must, blood would flow in this bitter quest.

Washington never responded directly to his critics, black or white. He was always too busy with the work at hand. But long after he was dead—and when he was still denigrated as an Uncle Tom by certain segments of his people—it was seen that a heedless battle for "rights" in

1895 might have meant the annihilation of the Negro race
by 1900. For this was a time when the day's burning question was whether the black man was actually human. As
one consequence, he was typically impoverished, un-
trained, and unled, with neither a clear understanding
of the political and social rights demanded in his name,
nor with even a glimmer of what he would do with them
should they suddenly be thrust upon him.

Labor, counseled Booker T. Washington, was the Negro's only salable commodity. Labor was the sure sole
means by which he could rise in this world. Far from
denying that colored men were entitled to an equal place
with whites, he deeply believed that they would irresist-
ibly achieve it. But first they had to survive. They had to
have something to barter for life's necessities. Given a
chance to exploit the manual arts, they would, in time,
learn to sell the products of their brains. And then there
would be nothing strong enough to hold them back, for
their time in history would have come.

So it was that Washington dedicated himself unspar-
ingly, not only to the comparative handful at Tuskegee,
but to all the thousands of pauperized farmers and their
wives and children in all the miles around. The school's
newly-organized agriculture department would teach the
latest farm techniques to the students—and would also
move out into the country to help "the man farthest down"
coax a useful crop from his scrimpy parcel of land. And
in October, 1896, the Institute paper reported that the
new department would be headed by a Mr. George W.
Carver, en route from Iowa.

George had once before been offered a faculty post
at another college. "I do not want to lose him from our

station staff here," Professor Wilson had then written. "Except for the respect I owe the professors, I would say he is fully abreast of them and exceeds in special lines in which he has a taste. We have nobody to take his place and I would never part with a student with so much regret as George Carver. These are warm words, such as I have never before spoken, but they are all deserved."

George stayed on at Iowa then, but the inevitable time of parting was soon come. Booker T. Washington's invitation was, to his heart and mind, a transcendent summons to duty. "To this end," he replied in acceptance of Tuskegee's offer of $1500 annually, "I have been preparing myself for these many years; feeling as I do that this line of education is the key to unlock the golden door of freedom to our people." In another letter to Washington, he wrote: "No individual has any right to come into the world and go out of it without leaving behind him distinct and legitimate reasons for having passed through it. I pray my work at Tuskegee become my reason for living."

Of course he knew of Dr. Washington's great work, and had been deeply moved by his speeches, and during that long summer of preparation and correspondence, he wrote to the principal: "I read your stirring address delivered at Chicago. I said 'Amen' to all you said. You have the correct solution of the 'race problem.'" No two more diverse men had ever traveled over widely divergent paths toward a linked destiny and a common goal.

In a misguided effort at persuading him to stay, someone pointed out to George that he would be earning more at Iowa than at Tuskegee, and could count on regular increases, as well. "That is not a consideration with me, sir," he said, and continued packing. There was a farewell party, subdued, tinged with the sadness of long farewell.

On behalf of the students and all the teachers, Professor Wilson presented George with a magnificent microscope. He took it and held it in his hands for a long time, studying it with beclouded eyes, and there was a mournful hush in the room as they watched him.

"All that I am," he said with painful slowness, "I owe to this place and to all of you. For that, more than for this beautiful gift, I thank you."

"Godspeed," they said. "Godspeed!" they called as he climbed up on the train that October morning and turned to wave. And then he was speeding south, leaving the Midwestern plains and prairies that had nourished him and brought him to manhood, bound south toward a strange land and, at last, toward that unknown star.

The rich fields fell behind and the red and yellow clays of Dixie stretched endlessly away from the train window. Soon they were passing through chaotic white puffs of cotton, a patch here and a plot there, and then great sweeping tracts out to the farthest horizon, and George Carver, for the first time, began to recognize the massive range of his task. This was the realm of King Cotton, and here before his eyes was the consequence of its tyranny, and nothing he had ever studied or heard about it had prepared him—nor could it have—for the staggering impact of countless humans, a whole people, paying homage to a mindless and unmerciful sovereign.

It was harvest time. Anyone who had the strength to raise a hand was in the fields picking cotton; women, children, backs bent under their huge, slowly filling sacks, and slowly moving along the everlasting rows, picking, picking. They straightened for a moment to watch as the train raced by, their black faces bereft of hope, their eyes lost in some mute and nameless longing, and then they stooped to pick some more. These, then, were his people, and George's heart ached with his compassion for them, and it sank at the enormity and apparent hopelessness of the work he had come to do. For he knew that what he saw from the train window was no different from what he would see if he traveled 1000 miles east or west or south —the same gullied fields and the same straggling fences, the same poverty-whipped people in the same shreds of overalls and jeans, drudging and struggling and suffering under the same swelling burden.

The cotton was planted up to the very doorways of their sad, unpainted shanties, chimneys sagging and roofs torn. Not a tree nor a flower nor a vegetable garden intruded on the domains of King Cotton, for cotton brought cash and nothing else mattered to the white landlord, nor even to the rare Negro who owned his own worn-out 40 acres. They could sell every bale they raised, nor could the black tenant farmer who tilled the white man's land, if he had been permitted to, have raised anything else. He had no machinery and often not even a mule. He knew nothing of vegetables or fruits or chickens or livestock. Cotton was all there was, although the money he was paid for his sad little crop was sometimes not enough to cover his debt at the landlord's store.

So cotton had ruled the South for 100 years, and year by year it had drained the good from the soil, producing an ever-smaller yield from the same enfeebled piece of ground, so that more fields had to be planted, and great forests felled to make room for still more fields. Without the trees' protective cover and binding roots, the topsoil was washed away by the decades' rains, and blown away by its winds, uncounted millions of tons of invaluable, irreplaceable plant nutrients eroded away to the sea and were gone forever. But in the memory of all living men, cotton had always been king, and what had to be had to be. So more trees were felled, and more land was planted to cotton, and an old farmer would spurn George Carver's counsel to try a different crop with the heartbreaking words, "Son, I know all there is to know about farming. I've worn out three farms in my lifetime."

George arrived at Chehaw, a railroad spur some three miles north of Tuskegee, early in the morning, October 8, 1896. When the train puffed and wheezed out of the little depot, he was absolutely alone, not a soul to be seen in the station, nor anywhere under the hot and dazzling bright sun. Unperturbed, he began strolling along the track, setting his bag down and bending sometimes to examine an unfamiliar weed. He was slim and wiry and slightly stooped as he walked with his eyes on the ground, and his eyes were dead black and benign, and his brow was wrinkled in thought. He wore high-laced shoes, a battered old cap and his baggy gray suit, the inevitable flower in his lapel, and he did not look much like the new Director and Instructor in Scientific Agriculture and Dairy Science. By the time a boy came clattering up to the depot in a buggy, he had collected an armful of Alabama plant life.

"Hey," the boy called, "you there on the track! You seen anything of a gentleman waiting for a ride to the Institute? A Mr. Carver?"

"I'm Mr. Carver," George said.

The boy's eyes snapped wide. "The teacher?" he gasped, and scrambled down from the buggy to snatch up the suitcase. "I—I'm sorry to be late," he stammered, "to keep you waiting. The horse . . ."

"I haven't been waiting," George said easily. "I've been getting acquainted with your growing things." He separated a sprig of green from his collection and held it out. "Can you tell me what this plant is?"

"Yes, sir," said the boy, eager to make amends by being helpful. "That's a weed."

George smiled. "So are they all. But every weed has a name and most of them have a purpose."

The boy backed away. "Yes, sir," he said dubiously, and threw the bag up into the buggy. Then they were riding up the old Montgomery road toward Tuskegee, past the cottoned-out farms and the propped-up cabins.

George strained to see over each rise and around every bend, anxious for his first view of the school. He imagined it as an oasis in this wasted land, a place of order and green fields, a place from which he could confidently venture forth to bring assistance to the people round about, and to which he could return for sustenance and inspiration. But even when the buggy pulled into the grounds of the Tuskegee Normal and Industrial Institute he could not realize that he had reached his destination; it seemed no different, unless a little worse, than the arid and forsaken countryside through which they had just passed.

The buggy stopped outside a bleak frame building and the boy said, "Here we are."

Appalled, bewildered, George climbed down. He turned from side to side, but wherever he looked there was only sand and bare yellow clay scarred by rain gullies so jagged and deep that a man—a horse!—could be lost in them. He spun back toward the driver in a kind of silent supplication, but the boy was already carrying his bag inside.

Drawn by some stupefying need to know the worst,

George walked numbly down the road. It lay ankle-deep in dust and would, he knew, run with a river of mud whenever it rained. Here and there neatly-lettered signs enjoined pedestrians to "Please Keep Off the Grass," but there was nowhere a blade of grass to be seen. He passed a pathetic collection of shacks and an occasional larger building, one of brick. In the sky behind Alabama Hall, an indolent circle of vultures took turns swooping down on the kitchen garbage flung out into a ditch. There was no sewage system.

His driver was calling, running after him. "Mr. Carver, sir!" he puffed when he had caught up. "Mr. Carver, Dr. Washington is waiting to see you."

The principal's office was a plain, sparsely-furnished room, but he so filled it with his vibrant presence that visitors rarely noticed the splintered desk and the bare floor. When he rose to greet the new teacher, the great burning force of the inner man added inches to his height and to the breadth of his shoulders.

"What do you think of our school?" he asked.

"There seems much to be done," was George Carver's reply.

"Yes, of course, but we can now believe it *will* be done." Washington leaned forward, eyes fiery with his vision. "Have you seen Alabama Hall, the four-story brick building? Can you imagine what it means to a Southern Negro to have such a place? Most of our students had never even seen a brick building, and now it is theirs and they are starting on another. They come to us from hovels, sir, and in the most abysmal ignorance, and we give them clean beds and teach them to make bricks, and to believe that if they can do that then nothing is beyond them." He rose and turned to look out of the room's single window. "Yes, there is much to be done," he said. "But we have made a start."

"You are doing remarkable work," George said. "I hope that I may be helpful."

It would not be easy. Washington told him that, as yet, his department was only a paper plan with a bare handful of students. The dairy consisted of a churn under a tree and, except for a few tools and an ancient horse, there was no equipment. A site had been chosen for an agriculture building, but for now he could be spared only a single room in Porter Hall. It would have to serve, as well, for his living quarters.

"It is a start. I will manage," George said.

"I pray to God you will. There is no more important work here than what you have come to do."

George walked out to the western edge of the school property where the new agriculture building would go up. Beneath the rise on which it was to stand, 20 starving acres had been set aside for farming. Beyond was a stretch of piney woods known by the students, with good reason, as Big Hungry, where some 30 lean, half-wild razorback hogs scrounged for enough food to stay alive.

He sat on a stump surveying his meager dominion. In Iowa now the hillsides would be green and the fields ripe and rich and bursting with their harvest. He could not help thinking about his greenhouse there, and the fine laboratories and modern equipment and the great herds of livestock. Now all he had with which to work these ruined fields were an ax, a hoe and a blind horse. "Here! That's enough of that!" he said aloud.

He took up a handful of the sandy soil and let it trickle through his fingers. Automatically a corner of his brain was deciding that it needed fertilizer, while the rest of his mind grappled with the larger problem. No good would come of indulging in self-pity, he resolved. If the good Lord had intended his life to be easy and uncomplicated, George Carver reflected wryly, He would not, for one thing, have made him a black man.

Tuskegee! Only yesterday the very sound of it had been filled with promise. Now, as he looked around him in a reddening sunset, he saw only challenge and need and a great testing time. Well, then, that must be enough, for him as for everyone who came to this place over the long, hard road that wound up from slavery. It was here, not in Iowa, that the salvation of his people would be wrought.

He remembered the faces he had seen from the train. He saw again the haunted eyes of the cotton-pickers, yearning only for enough to eat and a warm, dry place to sleep. Eighty-five percent of his people were desperately dependent on what they could wheedle from the soil, and so far they had neither the skills nor the strength to do more than barely survive. What were his petty needs, then, against their great collective hunger?

He rose. He would stay here and do the very best he could with whatever tools God saw fit to let him have. And suddenly cheered, uplifted, he started back toward his room, stopping once to pick a weed and study it. Then, noticing some young people on the dusty road up ahead, he hurried to catch up. "Excuse me," he said to them, "can you tell me what this plant is?"

VI. The Movable School

HE WANTED TO WRITE BULLETINS ON
FARM IMPROVEMENT, BUT WHAT GOOD
WERE BULLETINS TO FARMERS WHO
COULDN'T READ? SO HE MADE A "BULLE-
TIN" 20 ACRES ACROSS—THE SCHOOL
FARM. AND IF YOU LIVED TOO FAR AWAY
TO COME AND SEE IT, YOU COULD EXPECT
HIM IN YOUR FRONT YARD SOME SUNDAY
MORNING. "I'M FROM THE INSTITUTE,"
HE WOULD SAY. "MY NAME IS CARVER."
AND HE'D GET TO WORK.

—*Thomas M. Campbell*

Now HE was *Doctor* Carver, although rooting through
the rampant strawberry patch and tramping along Big
Hungry in a faded gray sweater, he looked more like
a field hand or, at best, a student assigned to farm chores
as punishment for some transgression of the rules. When
his boxes of books and materials arrived by freight, he
unpacked his microscope, but everything else remained
crated: there was not even space in that narrow room for
his precious mycological collection.

One morning he assembled his thirteen reluctant,
underfed students and announced that they were going
to build a laboratory. Whereupon he led them out to
the school junk heap and directed the reclamation of a
startling array of bottles, rusted pans, fruit jar lids,

113

saucepan handles, discarded flatirons, wire and odd bits of metal. No one had the vaguest notion of what this unaccountable teacher was about, but clambering light-heartedly over a mountain of trash seemed infinitely preferable to plowing and planting, and soon they were calling out, "How about this box, Dr. Carver?" And, "Can we use this pot?" And Dr. Carver almost never said no.

Having exhausted the possibilities of the school dump, the little band moved on into the town, scavenging the rubbish in back alleys and knocking on doors in a persistent hunt for rubber, old kettles and china jars. Then they bore their disparate hoard back to the Institute, and thirteen pairs of skeptical eyes watched as Carver fingered this tube and hefted that bottle. When at last he was conscious of their sharp scrutiny, he put down the bottle and showed them a wad of hopelessly snarled twine.

"This is useless," he said, "the result of ignorance." From the shelf behind him he produced a ball of salvaged and carefully-wound string and told them: "Here is intelligence." Gesturing then at the weathered odds and ends at his feet, he said, "Now all this may seem to be just junk to you. But it is only waiting for us to apply our intelligence to it. Let's get to work!"

An ancient kerosene lantern, cleaned and with its chimney lampblacked around a single pinhole, provided a strong focus of light for the microscope. An ink bottle with a piece of string stuck up through a cork for a wick served perfectly as a Bunsen burner. A heavy teacup became a mortar, a rounded stub of drapery rod the pulverizer. Into carefully labeled fruit jar lids went an assortment of chemicals. Chipped, scarred bottles were neatly cut down to size by burning string, to become beakers and retorts. Pieces of tin, holes punched in them with different-sized nails, turned into strainers through which soil samples could be accurately graded.

His boys watched in awe and astonishment, never again to doubt their teacher's resourcefulness, as the makeshift laboratory took shape. And this first lesson was perhaps the most valuable of all: in the years to come, when Tuskegee's graduates went out to remote sections and impoverished farms, they went armed with the knowledge that expensive and elaborate equipment was not a prerequisite for success.

So, with his scraps and discards, George Carver set out to remake the South. He began with his thirteen student farmers and he began at the beginning. He was not there to contribute to their individual gain, he said, nor was the school, but to help them lead their people forward. "That will be a mark of your success, not the style of clothes you wear, nor the amount of money you put in the bank. It is only service that counts."

He besieged the "office people" until they got him a two-horse plow—no one at Tuskegee had ever heard of such a thing—and on the morning it arrived he hitched himself up and beckoned the class to follow. The few who were tempted to giggle at the sight of the teacher from up North harnessed behind a pair of horses were promptly hushed by the others, who so vividly remembered the miracle of the laboratory. And none of them would ever forget Carver's high-pitched bidding to "Plow deep! Help those roots get down where the good is."

Before they could separate cream from milk, he had to teach them to assemble the separator, and clean it.

Instead of concentrating on tongue-twisting botanical names, he urged the class to just look at a plant, study it: "Soon you will see that the first thing to know about a sweet potato is that it is really a morning glory."

He had no use for the word "about," and told them so. A thing was either right or wrong, sufficient or insufficient. "You did not have to come all the way here to know that jumping *about* four feet across a five-foot ditch will only earn you a mud bath."

"Stop talking so much," he scolded the chatterboxes. "You never saw a heavy thinker with his mouth open." Again and again he attacked their contempt for farming by stressing life's fundamentals: "Learn to do the common things uncommonly well. We must always keep in mind that anything that helps fill a dinner pail is valuable."

He bore down hard on the relationship between soil, fertilizer and growth. "The ground can give back only as much nourishment as there is in it," he said, and astounded them with the revelation that there were other ways to feed the land besides with animal waste.

Among those in that earliest class was Jacob Jones, who went on to become a lawyer in Oklahoma, but who never forgot the years with Carver. "He taught me that the human brain—my brain!—held incalculable wealth, and all I had to do to free it was to want to."

J.H. Palmer stayed on at Tuskegee as a teacher all the rest of his life. Tom Campbell became the first Negro Field Agent in the United States Department of Agriculture. And Sanford Lee remembered Carver telling him that books about chickens and orchards and flowers were fine, but that if he walked among these things and looked and listened carefully they would tell him more than was in the books, for they spoke with the voice of God.

And so it was to be in class after class, generation after generation. An assistant who came to Tuskegee nearly forty years later to work in the old man's laboratory would afterward say that he was graduated from Cornell but educated by Dr. Carver.

For the year 1896, the 20-acre school "farm" yielded five scrawny bales of cotton and 120 bushels of sweet potatoes. A cup of strawberries a day and a gallon and a half of milk from the three cows was all anybody ever expected. The net loss for the year was $16.50. "They told me it was the worst soil in Alabama," Carver said, "and I believed them. But it was the only soil I had. I could either sit down and cry over it or I could improve it."

He prevailed on Washington to ask an Atlanta fertilizer company for a donation of several hundred pounds of phosphates for what was to be a three-year agricultural experiment. A letter, but no fertilizer, came back: "We sympathize with your desire but we want to be frank with you. There is only one colored man who is capable of conducting such scientific experiments on Southern soils. His name is George W. Carver and he is, unfortunately, in Iowa."

"We have Carver right here at Tuskegee," Washington wrote exultantly. "And it is he who is to conduct the experiments." The fertilizer arrived within the week.

Now every day, day after day, Carver was out with

his boys, dividing the 20-acre farm into sections, emphasizing the urgency of precise measurements and regard for the tiniest detail. "You are dealing with living matter," he reminded them. And always the injunction: "Plow deep!"

When the phosphate was spread, thinly covering what was now officially invested by the Alabama Legislature as a branch agriculture experiment station, the students were ready to plant a crop—but the teacher was not. "We have fed the ground only potatoes," he said. "Now we must go out and get the meat and greens." And they never forgot his pointed illustration of the soil's need for balanced nutrients. Nor could the South's tenant farmers expect any gifts of chemical fertilizer. If their experiment station was to truly justify the labor and high hopes going into it, they must use only materials available to everyone. And there *were* such materials, he said, an ideal fertilizer—right on the campus.

They were learning not to question Dr. Carver's outlandish pronouncements, but were surely nonplussed when he led them up still another trash mountain, this one to the north, well beyond Big Hungry, a dumping ground for tin cans, building sand, weeds and the bulkiest kitchen waste. From its midst sprang a magnificent pumpkin vine, runners winding extravagantly through the debris and and flourishing fine fat pumpkins. Tossed away with the garbage, unnoticed and untended, a single pumpkin seed had sprouted and taken root in the rich organic wastes, and the result was still another dazzling object lesson.

"There is no richer plant food than the things we ignore or throw away every day," Carver told the class, and off to the woods they went, to bring back buckets of leaf mold and muck from the hollows. Into a great improvised compost heap it went, and over it a layer of sandy soil, and over that every bit of organic waste that they could lay a hand on. Other students gaped as the neophyte farmers cried out in triumph at the discovery of a patch of weeds, or snatched a pail of vegetable peelings, grease or barn sweepings, and ran off with it to the compost pile. And in spring, when it had all rotted down to rich black humus, they spread it on their 20 acres.

From the first they had expected, quite naturally, to plant cotton on each square foot they had labored so hard to make arable and were consequently stunned when Carver decreed that their first crop would be, not cotton, but cowpeas. Cowpeas! All that backbreaking work for something that was fit only to be thrown to the hogs!

But cowpeas it was. Most plants, the teacher patiently explained to them, drained life-giving nitrogen from the earth—and cotton was among the most gluttonous consumers. But the legumes, of which cowpeas was one, had the unique ability to absorb nitrogen from the very air *and feed it back to the soil*. So still another essential fertilizer ingredient, worth 17 cents a pound commercially, could be gained at no cost.

The students were unimpressed. But what earthly good were cowpeas? they grumbled dispiritedly. And with the first harvest, Carver showed them. One evening the entire agricultural class was invited to a special meal cooked by their constantly-surprising teacher. They feasted on pancakes and potatoes and a succulent meat loaf—a blessed relief from their usual dinner of cornbread squares and salad greens—and when their bellies were full and the hails and huzzahs done with, Carver quietly announced that every last dish on the menu had been prepared from mashed cowpeas.

At the end of that first year, the farm, having provided for the Institute dining room well into November, showed a profit of $4 an acre. In the spring, demonstrating the efficacy of crop rotation, Carver had his boys plant sweet potatoes, and experimented with some other legumes— the soybean, a staple in China but virtually unknown in America; and an odd little vine he had seen out in the country that produced something called peanuts or, more often, goobers. It wasn't worth anything, and only a handful of farmers kept it, mostly because their children liked to crack the double-humped shell and eat the nuts.

The second-year production was 265 bushels of sweet potatoes an acre, more than six times the usual harvest. And when, finally, Carver did plant cotton, farmers, black and white, came to the experiment station and stared at the perfect stalks and plump bushes, some of which bore as many as 275 great white bolls. The yield was an incredible 500-pound bale per acre—so rich a crop had never been grown in that part of the land. Students and farmers were equally astounded. How could a Northerner, a schoolteacher who had never even *seen* cotton until he was a grown man, best those who had devoted a lifetime to raising it? And Carver's answer was always the same, always the essence of what he had been drilling into his class for three years: a plant needs certain things and the soil has certain things to give, and it is the farmer's job to make the right adjustment between them.

By 1897, the original 13 studying agriculture had become 76 and was the busiest group on the campus. In addition to a full schedule of classwork, there was the day-in, day-out business of running the ever-expanding farm—fences to build and mend, livestock to care for and crops to plant and harvest. And busier than any of the students was the new teacher. For these were Tuskegee's great growing years and as the lines of organization bent to accommodate the influx of new students and new ideas, chores not clearly earmarked for some other department wound up in agriculture. "Can you take care of this?" Washington would write with unfailing regularity, and Carver found himself designing the inside of the new agriculture building, testing well water, measuring rainfall and sending daily reports to the Montgomery weather bureau.

He resented none of these jobs, tackling each as though in all the world this was his only problem. But he was growing increasingly restive under the prickling of certain administrative irritants. One of these was the cramped quarters in which he was forced to live and work, and the other was the nagging and interference of what he called the "office people," among them Washington's older brother, John. Their views were parochial, their horizons constrained, and they were skeptical of the Yankee scientist from the moment he was hired. "We don't need a scientist," John Washington complained to his brother. "We need a dairyman." Carver's ideas about farming they deemed preposterous, and they hampered him in every way they could, finally taking to telling what must be planted and where, and holding back on the meager supplies due him when he ignored them.

Finally, in the spring, as part of his regular report to the principal, Carver had his say: "I still have no rooms even to unpack my goods," he wrote. "I beg of you to give me these, not for my sake alone but for the sake of education. At present the room is full of mice and they are into my boxes doing me much damage, I fear. While I am with you, won't you fix me so I may be of as much service to you as possible? I wanted a medical journal the other day in order that I might prescribe for a sick animal. It was, of course, boxed up and I couldn't get it . . . As to your office people, I do not mind them scoffing at my experiments, but you can see that I cannot have them deciding what is to be done and you will oblige me by telling them so."

Almost at once, both requests were granted. A second room was found for Carver's laboratory pending completion of the agriculture building, nor did anyone from the office ever again attempt to interfere with his work. For the fact was that no one valued Carver's contribution more than Booker T. Washington. Not only had he come to regard the agriculture teacher as the key to the entire Tuskegee experiment, but he was keenly aware that Carver's breathtaking common sense regularly brought savings and solved a host of problems in non-agricultural areas.

Once, overhearing the principal complain about the expense of a commercial bedbug exterminator which the school used in prodigious quantities—at $1.55 a gallon—Carver did some experimenting and reported to his chief: "I can make the bedbug exterminator for about 55 cents a gallon. The main difference is that I leave out the perfumery, which is rather costly. But as far as killing the bugs is concerned, it will kill them just as well." And of course it did.

The campus had always been treeless and bleak, and on ceremonial occasions pine branches were poked into the ground in an attempt at brightening the vista. But when withered these things were more cheerless than ever and, eventually, Washington asked Carver if he could plant some trees and properly landscape the campus. This he set about with genuine zest, grading and terracing, and putting out young shade trees and shrubbery and flowers so that, in time, the once barren fields would have the look and the mood of a great natural park.

One aspect of the overall plan defied Carver's best efforts. No matter how carefully he laid out the paths, students and faculty walked overland in a direct line for their destinations, tramping down the struggling young Bermuda grass and killing it. Finally, tired of depending on signs that were ignored, Carver stepped back and took a fresh look at the problem and there, sure enough, was the answer. And the grass flourished.

"How did you manage it?" Washington asked as they stood on a rise and looked out at the green and growing expanse before them.

"I decided that people are going to walk in a logical way," was the reply, "no matter how hard I try to persuade them otherwise. So I spent a few days watching their natural paths—and I put *my* paths under their feet."

He was pressed into service as an emergency veterinarian, prescribing for sick hogs, calving heifers and, one tense night, for Dr. Washington's horse, Dexter, after a guard had accidentally peppered it with shot. "I'd leave him be," Carver counseled. "It's only bird shot and has barely punctured the skin."

But Washington was devoted to his gray saddle horse and, after tussling with his conscience, apologized to Carver and sent to town for the white doctor. "Hmm," said Dr. Ludie Johnson after a thorough examination, "I'd leave him be. It's only bird shot and has barely punctured the skin."

Carver never changed his expression, but others in the small group watching promptly gossiped the word about that *their* Dr. Carver's treatment had been precisely the one recommended by the white doctor from Tuskegee—and the stock of *their* Dr. Carver soared.

His ways remained inscrutable though. He was forever puttering around in his crowded laboratory, testing, experimenting, studying soils and molds and insects, and everything that passed under his microscope was meticulously annotated and preserved. Walter Keys, a student assigned to tidy up Carver's rooms, tells of the Saturday morning the professor stopped him as he was about to dispose of a box of clayey soil. "But you've already tested this batch," Keys said, bewildered. "What good is it?"

"Look at it, boy!" was the answer. "What do you see?"

"Dirt. Just plain dirt." Keys had been looking at soil like this all his life and could not see how anyone could get excited about it.

"But what about the colors?" Carver insisted. "Have you ever seen such brilliant reds and yellows anywhere else? If a man could only extract those colors from the soil . . ."

Keys was looking at the teacher as though the poor

man had just separated from his senses. "But you can't do that," he said gently, as to a child. "Those colors are— are part of the dirt!"

And Carver replied, "Well, I don't know. I'll have to talk to God about this. Just don't throw any of it away."

His classes were awed by his uncanny ability to identify everything that grew or was, though of course they were just youthful enough to keep hoping that they would sometime stump him. Once they ingeniously fabricated a bizarre creature from the body of a beetle, the legs of a spider and the head of a giant ant. Barely able to suppress triumphant laughter, they thrust it at Carver and said, all innocence: "Look at this weird bug we found in the barn, Professor. What is it?"

But the laugh was Carver's. He took one look and said, "Why this is what we call a humbug."

George Carver would never forget his first graduation exercises at Tuskegee. Hundreds of parents and relatives came, by buggy and horseback and on foot, and they swarmed over the campus, asking their shy questions—"Was my Charles *good?* Did he *mind?*"—and gazing in wonder and reverence at the classrooms and machine shops and dormitories, at this miracle of a school which was all at once the fountainhead of their dreams and sacrifices.

Unlike the traditional commencement orator, Dr. Washington never mentioned success. "Go back to the place you came from," he told the stiffly proud graduates, "but don't waste your time looking for a paying job. If you can't get pay, ask for the privilege of working for nothing."

Dr. Carver took the principal's advice. He spent that summer writing a monograph on Alabama fungi, and contributed more than 100 specimens for a nationwide collection of grasses then being assembled by the Department of Agriculture. In July, he went himself to Washington to collaborate with the Pan-American Medical Congress in a study of medicinal flora in the United States. Many of the tried-and-true vegetable drugs long in use had grown scarce and now an effort was being made to catalogue them, and all other known plant remedies. Carver propounded dozens, many never before tried or even heard of, and in subsequent tests almost all were to demonstrate their curative value.

While in the Capital, he went to visit his old professor, James G. Wilson, only recently called to duty as the new Secretary of Agriculture by President McKinley. The two had a warm reunion, and when Wilson asked if there was anything at all he could do for his onetime pupil, Carver said that there was:

"I can think of nothing more important to Tuskegee than your endorsement of the work we are doing there. And I can think of no better way to make that endorsement clear to the country than by your presence on a visit. Can you come in the fall to dedicate our new agriculture building?"

Wilson hunched forward and, without a moment's hesitation, said, "You may announce it."

It was easily the most exalted and best-celebrated day in the 15-year history of the Institute. Never before had the Federal government taken official notice of the school, and never before had so high-ranking a dignitary set foot on the campus. Skyrockets lit the sky and the band played with joyful abandon, and there were two governors, a dozen mayors, judges, teachers, reporters and clergy in the audience of 5000 who came to hear

Secretary Wilson dedicate the gaunt new Slater-Arm-strong building to the pursuit of the agricultural arts. "I know, of course, that the study of agriculture is not just beginning at Tuskegee," he concluded, and looked straight at Carver when he said, "but surely it is now be-ginning in a new way."

It was to be supported in a new way. Carver had taken to walking over to Alabama Hall on Sunday evenings and sitting down to the ancient upright piano in the front parlor. The playing restored him, somehow. Without really thinking about the numberless and unending small difficulties of the week ahead, or the seemingly hopeless challenge of all the years to come, he gained strength for them by losing himself in the solace of music. And as he played his conscious mind remembered the faces and the voices of all his yesterdays—Aunt Susan and her plaintive question: "But don't you have enough learning, George?"; and Mariah Watkins, who had sent him into the world to give that learning back to their people; and Mrs. Payne, whose piano-playing had first roused in him that inde-finable longing, and the courage to hope that he might gain for himself a tiny corner in the beckoning world of beauty and knowledge; and Mrs. Milholland, who be-lieved in the thin, forever-needy youth with the patched jacket and the wildly improbable castles in air.

Would they be proud of him? he wondered. What would they think if they could see him in this poor, strug-gling school, trotting along behind a plow, striving to bring life to long-sterile acres, and a glimmer of light to the untouched minds of a few benighted youngsters, and all with the barest of resources and the most rudimentary tools? And his fingers fled over the keys as he played on.

Soon the students and some of the faculty began to

count on the Sunday evening "concerts," and they came
to stand quietly, or sit on the floor, lost in their own rev-
eries as Carver played *Swing Low, Sweet Chariot* and
Handel's *Largo* and the simple plantation melodies he
heard whenever his people came together at the close of
a long day, and he played as though he were alone in all
the world. When the night bell rang, they hurried off to
their rooms, but passing, sometimes stopped for a quick
word: "Oh, if my pa could hear your music. How he
loved . . ." And, "Once in our church a man came and
played the piano, but not so sweet." And one Sunday in
spring, the school treasurer, Warren Logan, said, "You
ought to play in the cities and towns, travel around—a
concert tour."

Carver laughed. "I'm a teacher, not a pianist."

"Dr. Washington is a school principal," Logan persisted, "not a public speaker. Yet he speaks all over the
country—raising money for the school."

It was true. Without Washington's vigorous skill with
words before audiences in Boston and Baltimore and
New York and Atlanta, crying out Tuskegee's promise
and beseeching funds for its very life, the Institute would
have long since been forced to close its doors and send its
students home. For a lasting moment the two men stood
face to face, and Carver was thinking how, with only a
little money, he could add 12 or 15 acres to the farm and
buy some more livestock, and perhaps even build a new
barn. And he said, "Can you arrange such a tour for this
summer?"

And Logan grinned. "It is already half-arranged."

The circulars said that Professor Carver of the Tuskegee Normal and Industrial Institute would appear in
concert. They were sent out to cities and crossroads ham-

lets in Alabama, Georgia, Louisiana and Texas, and were posted in town halls and colored churches and white schoolhouses. Somehow the money was found to buy, for the now-bemused teacher, a full-dress cutaway and vest and a pair of somber gray walking trousers—"It will be expected," Logan insisted—and, on July 8, 1899, he set forth. He played in Montgomery and Savannah and Baton Rouge, and in a countless string of small towns, each of which seemed to blur into the next as he moved on, riding the railroad coaches by day and playing by night. He played in public buildings and private homes, and sometimes in barns, and he played on grand pianos and battered uprights and, once, on a reed organ. In an east Texas town where, apparently, there had been a misunderstanding about his color, he was hooted from the piano bench before he could strike a note. But in a schoolhouse in Georgia, a white man and his wife came forward after the concert, and there were tears in their eyes, and they said that never before had they heard anything so moving, nor ever known that in music there could be such soul-stirring beauty. And each night, in a succession of pent and dingy hotel rooms, or huddled in the back of some rattling train, he counted the dimes and quarters and dollars, and when he returned to Tuskegee five weeks later, he had nearly $350. For years afterward the full-dress suit hung in his closet, never again to be worn, and when, now and then, someone asked about it, Carver would chuckle reminiscently and say, "Oh, that was from my career as a piano-player."

He had seen again the squalid homes and the grinding lot of his people. Wherever he went that summer, there were emaciated, hunger-haunted Negroes, often ten or

more in each tiny, tumbledown shanty, pigpens at their
very door, and the endless fields of cotton flaunting the
puny white bolls that were more important than humans.
He remained obsessed by the faces, by that look of abject
surrender they turned upon the world. It was as though
some inner voice had told them that it was useless to
strive or to hope, that their brief time on earth, and the
time of their children for all the generations to come,
was marked for adversity and pain.

But it need not be so! Long after the rest of the campus
was dark, Carver sat in his little room and pondered the
awful irony of want in a land that could be made fruitful
and productive, of dearth and despair and wanton waste,
all grown from ignorance, all within a stone's throw of
this hub of education. The soil was scorched and spent,
but it could be made rich! The despotism of King Cotton
could be ended. There could be good food for the bellies
of his people, and self-esteem for their souls, and opportunity for their children, if only they could be shown
that it was so!

The Farmers' Institute had been a tiny beginning. On
the third Tuesday of every month, farmers from the
nearby countryside, only a few at the start, shuffled self-
consciously into the immaculate new agriculture building. The proceedings would begin with a hymn. Then for
perhaps two hours, or for as long as he could hold their
attention, Dr. Carver would talk to them about their
land—how cotton had impoverished it and how corn-
stalks and leaf mold and kitchen wastes could restore it;
how all plants fed differently, some down deep and others close to the surface. If the same crop was planted on
the same piece of ground year after year, he said, the
soil never got a chance to rest.

He urged them to save out a small parcel for a kitchen garden. Fresh vegetables, costing only a few pennies for seed, would break the tyranny of the three M's—meat, meal and molasses—the time-rooted Southern diet that had made pellagra an unbidden and deadly caller in every home. Dramatically, then, he would cut into a ripe red tomato—universally regarded as poisonous—and to the accompaniment of horrified gasps, eat it with obvious relish. "You will please notice that I have not died," he said and went on to explain that tomatoes could be a prime protection against scurvy.

He then led them out to the experiment station. There, spread before their eyes, was the living proof of everything he had told them: huge cabbages and onions seven inches across, larger than had ever been grown anywhere, fine, juicy cantaloupes and watermelons, and a fantastic yield of white potatoes. The per acre profit had soared to $75. Carver showed them how the cowpeas had enriched the soil—"It would cost $25 an acre to buy the good this puts into the earth for nothing," he said—and how its roots loosened the ground to let water and air in. For those who could read, he prepared a bulletin listing 18 ways of cooking cowpeas. For those who couldn't, he patiently recited each recipe until the light of understanding shone in their eyes and they exclaimed, "Yes, yes! Now we got it, Professor!"

The scrubby handful with whom the Farmers' Institute had been launched grew to 25, 50, even more. Farmers who suddenly realized that their neighbors were growing bigger melons and better cotton wanted to know why, and the next third Tuesday they, too, came to Tuskegee. They brought their wives and little ones, and when the day's lessons were done they camped on the parade ground and ate the savory food prepared by student cooks and sang the full-fraught melodies of their haunted past.

But they were so few. Out there, where the roads ended, in the thickets and the swamps, there were thousands of Negro families, day laborers and share-croppers and tenant farmers, none of whom had so much as heard of Tuskegee, and all of whom lived, as had their forebears, on the ragged edge of survival. Carver had seen them, and now he was determined, somehow, to reach them. Nor would it be enough to *tell* them what to do; he must *show* them.

Somewhere he wheedled a wagon and a mule, and with a few tools, seed packets sent down by Secretary Wilson, and some boxed demonstration plants, he set forth after classes one Friday evening. The first movable school was going to the people. In years to come it would be replaced by a specially-built rig, and that by a motorized van, and the idea would spread across the South so that soon dozens of movable schools were fanning out across the land, carrying to the poorest of God's creatures the startling word that their lives could be better and more meaningful. But none of the fine and fully-laden trucks and trailers was ever to be as important as the creaky little wagon George Carver drove into the shadowed woodlands that Friday in 1899.

He had no illusions about persuading the people to abandon cotton as a cash crop. He could say to them that it ruined their land and kept them in fetters, but they asked him how else they could pay their debts? Even the suggestion that they rest a portion of their land met with sullen resistance. "Do you remember how much fuller the cotton bushes were when you were children?" he said. "Look at them now—you won't get six bales from this whole farm! The land is tired, like a man who's been bent over harvesting all day. It needs a rest."

And they looked down and scuffed at the dusty earth, and one said, "I know the land is tired, Professor. I *been* knowing it, and so have we all. But what happens to us and our young 'uns while our land rests?"

And he passed among them a sweet potato from the experiment station. "Put ten acres in yams and you'll have nourishing food for your table the year round, and the vines and culls and peelings will feed your hogs." They could grow two sweet potato crops a year, he told them, and still do the soil less damage than would a single planting of cotton. And in three years, if they went back to cotton, those same ten acres would produce at least five full bales.

They listened grudgingly, and made no promises. It was a time when most of the rural people still believed in "signs" and voodoos, and the peculiar counsel of this school-man seemed puny indeed against the age-old rituals and the black arts.

"Your chickens are sick because no sunlight gets into that coop to dry it out," Carver told a farmer.

"No, sir," was the response. "They's sick because that brown 'un there was hatched on a full moon and he's done put a hex on the others."

He kept traveling and he kept talking. Every weekend, every moment he could spare, he rode that jolting wagon up and down Macon County, seeking out isolated farmers, cornering groups at fairs and on street corners of a Saturday afternoon. He talked to men who stared blankly back at him, uncomprehending and uninterested, and to others who mocked him—"How come you smarter'n me? You just as black."

But there were others who listened, and some who asked questions, and a few who memorized every word he uttered because they couldn't read the bulletins he'd brought to distribute. He showed them the huge cabbages and onions from the experiment station—"We grew these on the worst 20 acres in Alabama!"—and he taught their wives how to cook cowpeas, and little by little they came to see some sense in what he said.

"You the school-man?" asked a weather-beaten old soul who'd come slogging through the darkening thickets to find him. "My woman and me'd be proud to have you spend the night with us. This way."

He slept in their cabins, usually on a cleared patch of floor, and ate at their tables, although he always contributed a sack of fresh vegetables, and often the meat. They worried that he might be lofty and commanding, as would befit a man with so much learning, but his ways were simple and his words direct, and they were soon at ease. They liked him for he listened to them. And in the long evenings of talk, they painlessly absorbed some of his most valuable lessons, and sometimes in unexpected ways. One morning the young son of his hosts saw him brushing his teeth at the water pump and, thinking that the school-man had thrown a fit and was frothing at the mouth, would have run screaming for help if Carver, spluttering, had not managed to convince him that all was well. Not one to pass up an opportunity, the professor then explained the virtues of scrubbed teeth to the lad and presented him with a toothbrush. Thereafter, whenever they met, the boy rewarded Carver with a fixed and dazzling white smile.

He rode on. Where farmers followed the traditional practice of burning off weeds and last year's stalks, he told them that what they were doing was no different from burning off the outside bills on a roll of greenbacks. "Turn it under," he said. "It may be a little more work, but next spring you can put those bills in your pocket." Where the winter rains had leached away the topsoil and laid bare gravel and hardpan, he urged them to put in a ground cover: "Plant peanuts—they're good for your children and for the land, both."

He pressed them to save five cents every single working day. At the end of a year, they would have accumulated $15.65—which would pay for three acres of land and leave a reserve fund of 65 cents. There was no other way to break the grip of the landlord or the plantation commissary, he said. They smiled secretly at this—the Saturday temptations of the town were impelling and vivid the week long—and took to calling one old codger "Crazy" Chauncey because he was stubbornly heeding the school-man's advice. But then a year passed and "Crazy" Chauncey bought his three acres and now he was Mister Chauncey. And all over Macon County nickels were suddenly being hoarded in jars and tins and hollowed tree stumps.

Slowly, doggedly, Carver transformed the eating habits of the South. Though hogs were prime in summer, they had never been butchered before the first freeze—until the professor taught the farmers how to cure the meat so that, even in the hottest weather, it wouldn't spoil. Long before the medical profession understood the value of raw fruit as a safeguard against nutritional diseases, Carver, wherever he went, was advocating that wild plums and apples be made part of the daily diet. He handed out Secretary Wilson's seed packets, but persuading the farmers to start a vegetable garden was only half the job; their wives had only the most meager idea of what to do with the produce. So, sleeves rolled, Carver patiently demonstrated techniques of flavoring and cooking the greens and beets and potatoes. He reminded the people that good food from their gardens, properly prepared, could keep the larder full all through the long winter, and he brought them jars for pickling and canning, and showed them how vegetables spread in the sun and dehydrated would keep for months.

Waste was a noxious foe in every yard and kitchen, and Carver turned on it all his awesome ingenuity, goaded by a stinging distress at the incongruity of his people's pinched and barren existence, and the prodigality with which they squandered resources close at hand. They threw away enough hog fat to keep each family in soap all through the year. Sweet potatoes too stringy to eat could be grated into superior starch, and Carver showed them precisely how. Pine needles, cheese cloth and burlap were woven into mats and coverings, and brightened homes where brightness of any kind had been alien and unknown. He gave them azalea slips and pansy seeds and said, "Plant these in your dooryard. A flower is God's silent messenger." And he rode on.

In the spring of 1899, there had come to Tuskegee a young man who, under Carver's fortifying direction, was to advance the movable school to the attainment of its ultimate objectives. His name was Thomas M. Campbell and he had run away from his father's house in Athens,

Georgia, and tramped the 200 miles to Tuskegee, though his older brother, a senior, had written to warn him of a smallpox epidemic at the Institute. "I do not mind the smallpox," Tom Campbell wrote back in ignorant seriousness, "since it is small," and set out. He arrived barely in time to exchange a last word with his stricken brother.

"Let them bury me here," the dying Willie Campbell said, "and you stay on. And whatever work you decide to do, don't ever let any other man do more of it than you."

Heartsick, lost, Tom stumbled around the bewildering campus. Somehow he found himself wandering near the experiment station and there chanced on a tall, sad-eyed man in a faded gray sweater. They talked, walking along until the sun reddened and then vanished behind Big Hungry, and George Carver comforted the frightened, penniless boy, and assured him that he would be allowed to stay at the school. A way would be found for him to work out his tuition.

"What trade would you like to study?" Carver then asked. "Farming?"

"No!" All his life Tom Campbell had seen the colored people humped over in the cotton fields, and he had come to believe that that was all they were fit to do. But here at Tuskegee his brother had been learning barbering, and over the hill there were Negroes in the sawmill, and others in a carpentry shop and a smithy. He had watched them with astonishment and envy, and now he thought he would like to try one of those trades.

"I see," said Dr. Carver thoughtfully. But he had not yet given up on this somber lad to whom he had taken an instant liking. There was a chronic shortage of good people for his classes—students instinctively shied away from what they assumed was the same drudgery they'd always known—and this one, Carver believed, could be exceptional. And very casually he asked, "How about agriculture? Do you think you might like that?"

Tom tried this bizarre new word on his tongue. "Agriculture," he repeated, and anxious to conceal his ignorance, committed himself without further ado. "Yes!" he said. "That's what I want to learn—agriculture!"

And so the die was cast. Nor was Tom Campbell ever to regret his impromptu decision, for agriculture as taught by Dr. Carver was not at all like the scrabbling farm life he had known. And just as Carver sensed, Tom had the intuitive capacity for grasping not only the "how" and "what" of things, but the all-important "why," as well. Soon the thin teacher and the robust young man were riding the Tuskegee wagon together, plodding through the outback every weekend, and steadily widening the scope and services of the movable school.

That first buggy had carried only a plow and a few smaller implements. Now, into a triple-tiered and covered wagon especially designed by Carver went a cow, which was milked wherever a group could be gathered, and a cream separator and churn, whose operations were patiently explained and demonstrated at each such stop. It would be some time before the rural people could aspire to a cow or a separator, but Carver believed that every man should have something useful to work toward. "Our job is to make them want a cow," he told Tom. "Their job is to earn one." Meanwhile, he carried, too, a razorback and a plump purebred hog so they could actually see the difference between them. And before long the ubiquitous razorback began yielding to a finer, fatter breed.

One place the itinerant teachers could always count on finding an interested group was outside the local church on Sunday morning, for in God's house the burdened colored folk always found a measure of solace. Carver and Tom, then, would listen to services and rush out immediately afterward to stand ready by their exhibits, and soon a lively crowd had pressed close and the demonstrations would begin. Though there were sometimes difficulties. For among what Booker T. Washington called "the present army of rural pastors," there were many who were poorly prepared for their responsibility and had no realistic understanding of their people's social and economic needs. They would send them home from church with instructions to spend the afternoon "prayin' and contemplatin'," and one ended the service once by proclaiming, "I see the Tuskegee wagon outside and am obliged to tell you that we can't afford to engage in worldly affairs while we are busy saving souls!"

Other servants of God were more far-sighted. Invited by Carver to spend a few days with the movable school, the Reverend L.W. Owens wrote to his wife: "At 8 everyone was in work clothes. There was a class in terracing, another learning to make and apply whitewash. Others were learning rug-making, egg-candling and care of the sickroom. Next morning I borrowed a pair of overalls and learned a few things myself."

As word about the Tuskegee wagon spread through Macon County, Carver and his ardent helper began attracting goodly Saturday afternoon crowds to the town squares, or at the courthouse steps. At first the whites were uneasy with such an arrangement and, indeed, sometimes roughly broke up the meetings altogether.

"We don't want uppity niggers around here," they said, and meant that they did not want colored farmers out-producing the white ones.

Carver practised Booker T. Washington's devout conviction that, "You can't keep a man in the ditch unless you're willing to get in with him." Before long the white men quit grumbling and edged close to hear what "the nigger teacher" was saying. And Carver was gratified to have them. Blacks and whites in the South had the same problems, the same needs. He was dropping a stone into a vast sea of darkness and the more people, black or white, he could help to a better sweet potato yield, or a better life, the farther out would the ripples of light spread.

To everyone he offered his "magic" formula: "Start where you are." Everywhere he repeated his live-at-home precept—"A good garden will free you from the plantation store!"—and strove everywhere to make the home more attractive and to stir the people's pride of possession. He demonstrated how three steps were safer, better-looking and easier to make than the traditional log doorstep that had to be cut in the woods and dragged all the way back. He showed the men how to build a sanitary toilet and the women how to sew curtains, weave rugs and set an appealing table. And returning to Tuskegee one evening, in those final minutes before dusk, it came to him that they had at hand the means for covering their worn and weather-beaten shanty-houses with fresh, clean color—at no cost!

He and Tom were clip-clopping slowly across a rise of ground and on every side great banks of clay, caught in the sun's last radiance, gleamed back at them in creamy hues of red and yellow and blue. "God would

not have made such colors for no purpose," he said, half
to himself, and Tom mumbled an automatic, "Yes, sir."
It had been an arduous weekend and the boy was nearly
asleep. But George Carver was abruptly wide-awake
with inspiration. He trusted beyond doubt in the biblical
injunction, "I will lift up mine eyes unto the hills from
whence cometh my help," and he understood it to mean
that to find his succor, man must search for it with all
his energy and with every resource of his mind. And
now Carver searched, racking his brain, thinking, thinking.

When finally they got back to the campus late that
night, he dragged out his boxes of clay and studied
them, sifted the rough, color-laden texture through his
fingers, and waited resolutely for God's message. Toward
dawn, when it came, it was direct and simple and
crystal-clear. He had strained the sand from a shovelful
of yellow clay through a gunnysack and poured what
was left into a bucket of water. Now, only minutes later,
the water showed clear again. He poured it off carefully
and saw in the bottom of the bucket a durable and
dazzling bright yellow wash paint.

As was his custom, Carver was out in the woods before daybreak. But on this day he sought no uncommon
plant specimens. Exhausted and profoundly grateful, he
had come out to thank the Lord for His help, and having
done so he walked alone in the warmth of the new day
and reflected, not on his discovery, but on how he would
put it to use. He resolved that wherever he went from
now on he would dig some clay out of the nearest bank,
and show the people how easy it was to make wash
paint. And they would paint their poor houses, inside
and out, and feel another spark of achievement and

pride, and all over the South the man farthest down could take another tiny upward step.

And that was how it was. It is said that Dr. Washington, riding down a country path where he had visited for years, failed to recognize the trim, freshly-painted shanties and cabins as the bleak little community he had always known. He returned elated to pump Carver's hand in fervent congratulation. Then he said, "But will the colors last?"

And Carver pointed to the shining hills beyond the parade ground and said, "They have lasted there for 1000 years. I daresay they will last another 30 or 40."

The movable school was to become a worldwide institution. From that first rickety, mule-drawn cart it evolved, in June 1906, into the Jesup Agricultural Wagon, a fully-equipped traveling experiment station, the funds for which were donated by Morris K. Jesup, a New York philanthropist. In 1918, the state of Alabama provided a huge automobile truck and Tom Campbell, now a United States Agricultural Collaborator—the first Negro to hold so high a post in the South—journeyed even farther afield, bringing his tools and exhibits into areas long bypassed by the rush of the years. A practical nurse—who became Mrs. Campbell—was added to the entourage, and while Tom directed classes in animal husbandry and tree-spraying, she gathered the women about her and demonstrated sound practices in baby care and sanitation and nutrition. And the ultimate place of the movable school is best marked by the fact that when the first truck finally wore out and the state could offer no money for a replacement, the farmers of Macon County put up dimes and dollars totaling $5000 to buy and equip a new and even larger school on wheels.

Meanwhile, requests from other counties and communities poured in on Tuskegee for assistance in launching their own movable schools. And Carver sent them instructions and exhibits, and sometimes rode along on their earliest trips. Inevitably the idea spread to lands across the seas, and visitors came to the Institute from Russia, Poland, China, Japan, India and Africa. All were referred to Dr. Carver, and all listened, enthralled, as the lanky, unassuming professor recounted his experiences in the rural South and suggested techniques for adapting them abroad.

To his dying day, Carver would believe that the movable school had been his most important work. From that small beginning sprang a nationwide revolution in soil conservation, the curse of pellagra was all but eradicated and millions of his people could lift their eyes to the sun. And all this would forever be symbolized for him by the memory of a poor old sharecropper thrashing through the dark woodlands until he found the school-man and said, "My woman and me'd be proud to have you spend the night with us."

VII. "Mr. Creator, Why Did You Make the Peanut?"

I CAN GIVE MY BOY A SACK OF PEANUTS
TO TAKE TO THE FAIR, YES, BUT WHAT
CAN I DO WITH A WHOLE WAGONLOAD?

—*Unknown Macon County Farmer*

IN A REPORT to Dr. Washington dated January 20, 1904, Carver summarized his daily activities, as follows:

"Today my classes run thus: from 8:00 to 9:00, agricultural chemistry; 9:20 to 10:00, the foundation and harmony of color to the painters; 10:00 to 11:00, class of farmers, and one period more in the afternoon. In addition to this I must try—and rather imperfectly—to overlook seven industrial classes scattered here and there over the grounds. I must test all the seeds, examine all the fertilizer—based upon the examination of the soil of the different plots. I must also personally look after every operation of the experiment station and write up our work, distribute it, and keep in touch with all experiment stations. I must endeavor to keep the poultry yard straight. In addition to the above I must daily inspect 104 cows that have been inoculated, looking carefully over the temperature of each one, making comparisons and prescribing whatever is necessary, besides looking after the sickness of other animals."

145

Now in his eighth year at Tuskegee, he declined a raise in salary, as he was to do consistently throughout his long tenure. When he died in 1943 he was still earning the same $125 a month offered by Washington in that fateful letter dispatched to Iowa with prayerful hope in the long ago spring of 1896. The fact was that Carver no longer had the slightest regard for money. Once it had been his latchkey to learning, a necessity along the road the good Lord decreed he must travel. Now he had reached his destination. His simple needs were met. And time and again harried Treasurer Logan had to plead with him to cash his paychecks so the school's books could be balanced. Chided once by a fellow teacher for turning down a salary increase, Carver, genuinely baffled, said, "What would I do with more money? I already have all the earth."

The painting class had been his own idea. He taught his students to mix an astonishing array of colors from native clays, made them canvases from the pulp of crushed peanut shells, frames from corn husks, and gave his own hauntingly beautiful pictures—most of them painted with his fingers—to anyone who even casually admired them. For the first time he was among his own people, and though he missed the intellectual stimulation of his old friends back North—and maintained a lifelong correspondence with the Milhollands, Miss Budd and his former teachers at Iowa State—his commitment to the little Tuskegee community seemed to leave no time for regret.

He walked often in the colored district, chatting with children and old folks, bringing plants for the ladies and diagnosing the ills of their flower beds. The streets began to brighten perceptibly, and when Carver planted rows of cedars along the sidewalks' edge, the town of Tuskegee took on the look of shaded grace that characterizes it to this day.

Sometimes the white people sent to ask his advice about their gardens, and he always gave it unstintingly. A flower, he believed, did not "belong" to anybody but God, and he was bent on helping as many as he could to fullest beauty no matter where they happened to be growing. Occasionally, though, his patched sweater and shapeless cap deceived even perfectly-intentioned whites into addressing him as a handyman or beggar. Once, a lady who had sent for "the Tuskegee man" to look at her ailing peach trees saw a poor and somber-looking Negro approaching and asked if he would like to earn 50 cents: her grass needed cutting. Something held Carver silent —perhaps his innate reluctance ever to distress anyone; perhaps the prickling memory of days when a lawn-mowing job meant he would eat that night—and he went at once to the mower and neatly cut the grass, front and back. Then he knocked on the door and said, "Now what seems to be the trouble with your peaches, Ma'am?"

Another time a man noticed Carver pulling some unusual weeds from his front yard and decided that the poor old fellow was preparing to eat them. "They grow lots bigger out back, Uncle," he called. "Help yourself." And was probably greatly gratified when Carver thanked him and went out back to gather a huge armful.

At school, of course, there were no such problems. Next to Washington himself, Carver was soon the most familiar figure on the campus and there was little he did—climb a tree to check for blight; dig a drainage ditch all by himself; tether a cow outside his window so he could watch its reaction to an inoculation while working on soil samples—that still surprised anyone but the rankest newcomers. He was a special favorite of the lady teachers, who regularly took him to task over his ancient wardrobe, saw to it that he got something to eat when, as often happened, he worked right through mealtime—and were fashionably flattered when he expressed shy thanks by bringing to their table in the dining hall a magnificent bouquet of weeds and wildflowers.

His social life was severely circumscribed by an absolute dedication to his work that took no account of the hour of the day, the day of the week or the season of the year. He began to teach a Sunday evening Bible class, sometimes went on a trip to lecture—usually to another college—and, on Thanksgiving and Christmas, was a dinner guest of Tom Campbell's new family. Otherwise the laboratory and the experiment station filled George Carver's life, and he seemed to shrink from anything that would have made it different.

Mrs. Campbell remembers a Christmas evening when the usually subdued and serious teacher lost himself in play with her children, one of whom had been named for him. He brought them a top-like toy of his own devising and, while they howled with glee—and Carver cackled triumphantly—spun it again and again, crawling under the tree to retrieve it, and spinning it once more. Later, propped against a sofa with a youngster on each knee, he told them a bedtime story about a little boy who could talk to the flowers. When at last they were tucked in and Tom was busy in the kitchen, young Mrs. Campbell softly said, "You have a good way with children, Professor Carver. You ought to have a family of your own."

He smiled, perhaps a little ruefully. "What woman would want a husband forever dropping soil specimens all over her parlor? How could I explain to a wife that I had to go out at 4 o'clock every morning . . ."

"Oh, the right woman would understand!"

". . . to talk to flowers?"

They both laughed, but Mrs. Tom Campbell never forgot that little talk. And George Carver never married.

Though there was once, in fact, a girl he must have cared for deeply. It is a corner of his story rarely probed and never before fully told, and its poignant ending is fraught with what-might-have-been. Miss Hunt was a teacher in the home economics department, remembered by the handful still living who knew her as small and pert and as full of high spirits as Carver was imbued with his life's work. Each was caught by the particular quality of the other—Carver by her vivacity, Miss Hunt by his dedication—and they became regular dining companions and walked together across the campus, oblivious to it and to all who passed, deep in conversation or magically-shared silence.

It did not last long. In his characteristically methodical way, Carver must have assessed every aspect of the matter, and it is not hard to imagine him, Lincoln-like, tortured by the need to make a decision that, one way or the other, had to end in cruelty and pain, struggling toward an almost-predestined answer. He was well past forty years old. If he was ever to marry, it must be now, and to this girl. But was he worthy of her? Of any woman who expected—and had a right to expect—

devotion and concern and deepest family feeling? In his innermost heart, George Carver knew that his first loyalty was and would always be to his work. He had no interest in money, which might be all right for him but could be fatal to a marriage. And finally this was the time when he was absorbed in the movable school. He could hardly see himself playing the happy husband, at home every weekend, when out where the street lights ended and the woodlands began there were people who needed him, not to be happy, but to survive.

There were days then when no one saw much of George Carver. He walked in the woods, or shut himself up in his narrow room. Without explanation, he failed even to appear at his classes for the first of only two times in all his years at Tuskegee. And then, apparently, he knew what he had to do. There was no dramatic confrontation. There were, perhaps, a few awkward, regretful words, and not long after Miss Hunt left Tuskegee. So it was that Carver made the choice: his life would be full, but never complete, his time on earth enriching, but not enriched.

Early in the 1920s—when Carver was deeply immersed in a project of even more significance than the movable school—he had word that Miss Hunt, who never married either, was dead. And that was the second time he failed to appear for his classes.

In the Main Street square of the little Alabama town called Enterprise, perhaps 90 miles south of Tuskegee, there stands an astonishing monument: it immortalizes one of the most devastating agricultural scourges of modern times.

"In profound appreciation of the boll weevil and what

it has done," reads the legend. "As the herald of prosperity, this monument was erected by the citizens of Enterprise, Coffee County, Alabama." Much bitterness built that grim memorial, and a private agony of soul for George Carver.

The boll weevil is a dark, rapacious little creature less than a quarter of an inch long. It feeds on the cotton plant, then infests it with millions of microscopic eggs. Around 1892 it slipped into Texas from Mexico and in the next 25 years laid waste field after great cotton field across all the old Confederacy. Its annual toll soon exceeded $100 million. No one can say how many lives it blighted. To the luckless legions of farmers in its ravaging eastward path through Louisiana and Mississippi and Alabama, the weevil brought ruin, an end to every hope. In 1915, not one Coffee County farmer in ten could pay his tax bill, and Enterprise, the county seat, was a ghostly presence in the midst of the endless reaches of mutilated cotton, its stores shuttered in bankruptcy, its people destitute and lost.

"Burn off your infested cotton!" Carver had beseeched the desolated farmers wherever he went. "Plant peanuts!"

But no one listened. "Plant peanuts?" snorted a grizzled old sharecropper in response to Carver's pleas. "What for? Cotton's important—it makes clothes; everybody needs clothes. But peanuts! Why, man, give me 120 acres and I'll grow you enough peanuts to do the whole state of Alabama!"

It was quite true. Peanuts were only a children's treat and Carver had not at first been greatly concerned with any other uses to which they might be put. He knew only that they were a nutritious food, and that they could

restore the land—and that there had to be something
in God's great garden that would flower in the doomed
cotton fields. To that quest he had bent every effort,
searching, testing, working against time as the dark
cloud from Texas grew larger and came closer.

As early as 1906 he was warning that the insidious
spread of the boll weevil could not be stopped. At best,
an especially robust strain of cotton, planted and harvested early, might escape the worst of its lash. He had
developed four new long-fibre, wilt-resistant types, and
identified several until-then mysterious cotton diseases,
one of which bears his name. But he remained convinced
that, in the end, only another crop would save the small
farmers from ruin. He continued to urge the cowpea and
sweet potato on them, but if they raised any at all it
was only enough to fill their own needs. To new purpose,
he picked up his experiments with the Chinese soybean
which, in all the nation that year, only a few of the old
hands at Iowa State had ever even heard of. And though
it was easily grown and transmuted into flour, meal,
even milk—and, thanks to these early efforts, would
someday become a Southern staple—Carver soon realized that the time was not yet when the parochial
Alabama farmers would give up precious cotton acreage
to this odd and frighteningly unfamiliar plant. And so
he came, at last, to the peanut.

Through its known record of 3000 years in all the
earth's sub-tropical lands, the peanut has been variously
called the ground pea, pindar, monkey nut, goober nut
and ground nut. It came to North America in the slave
ships of the eighteenth century—goober is one of the
few African words still retained in the English language
—and this is one of history's special ironies: brought to

the New World by the slave traders because it was the cheapest of all foods for the millions of Negroes needed to serve the cotton empire, the peanut, 150 years later, became the instrument by which cotton's economic deathlock on slavery's heirs was finally broken.

Actually it is not a nut at all but an herb, closely related to the cowpea, and develops beneath the ground like a potato. It demands little from the soil, absorbing nitrogen from the air and storing it against future need. Through the longest dry spells the plant patiently marks time, sprouting swiftly ahead when the rains finally fall. Then the stems lengthen and bend, pushing seed pods into the ground where they ripen to mature nuts that have only to be pulled up and dried, dozens to each cluster.

"Nothing that grows that easy can be any good," farmers said, and Carver set out to show them otherwise. His Bulletin Number 31 listed 105 peanut recipes and the best techniques for cultivation and harvest. He pointed out that there was more high-protein nourishment in a pound of peanuts than in a pound of the best beefsteak. And to the owner of every decimated cotton field he brought the same cheerless but urgent advice: the blighted cotton had to be burned or plowed under, the soil sprayed and left fallow for a month. Then it would be ready for peanuts.

To dramatize his campaign he persuaded Washington to invite nine influential Macon County businessmen to lunch at the Institute. The meal, prepared by the senior girls under Carver's direction, consisted of soup, mock chicken, a creamed vegetable, bread, salad, ice cream, candy, cookies and coffee. Everything on the menu was made from peanuts; everything had a unique and zesty flavor. When finally Carver announced his deception to the guests, informing them that they had had nothing but peanuts prepared in nine different ways, they laughed in disbelief at his little joke, then looked at each other sheepishly and burst into spontaneous applause.

And slowly, pushed by the weevil and pulled by Carver, the people began to do as he said. Where there had been random, neglected peanut patches tucked into otherwise useless wedges of ground, now there were 20- and 40-acre fields dominated by the velvety plant and its shy white flower. Soon peanuts were the number one crop in a great farming belt that ran from Montgomery to the Florida border, then began pushing north as whole communities abruptly abandoned cotton.

And then—calamity, this time in the seemingly innocent question of an old lady, a widow, who timidly knocked on Dr. Carver's laboratory door one early October afternoon. She had read his bulletins and followed his instructions faithfully, and her worn-out farm had responded with a bumper crop. Now, having set aside all the peanuts she and her hired man could conceivably use in the year ahead, she still had hundreds of pounds left over. And she asked, "Who will buy them from me?"

And Carver had no answer. So engrossed had he been in staving off the evils of the one-crop system, so successful was he in promoting the peanut, that almost alone he had created a monster as cruel and unforgiving as the weevil itself. One hasty trip into the countryside and his blunder glared back at him from every farmyard. He saw barns and storehouses piled high with the surplus, and in many places peanuts rotted in the field—what was the sense in harvesting them? And farmers came to ask him what to do, and some cursed him, and he returned to his laboratory racked with gloom and guilt.

It was simply not in his nature to say—even to himself —that it was not his problem, that he had fulfilled his responsibility by giving the peanut to the farmers, and let someone else worry about where they could sell it. His responsibility had no easy limits, and for days he tormented himself that, smug and heedless, he had thought the problem only halfway through. The people needed to be liberated from their slavish dependence on cotton, yes, and they needed a wholesome, easy-to-grow food, and peanuts filled both these essentials. But they had to have a cash crop, too, for clothing and farm implements and self-respect, and he could not believe that God would have opened his eyes to the peanut, and sent the boll weevil to help him give it a start, without some grand design that would provide for *all* the needs and hungers of His children. Therefore the fault must lie with him, God's imperfect servant, George Carver. And if there were no markets for peanuts, then he, George Carver, would have to find them.

Years later, when he was world-famous and bent with years, Carver traveled to St. Paul, Minnesota, to talk to the students at Macalester College. And to these young people he told the poignant story of this, his single most crucial undertaking.

Heartsore and beset by the inexplicable contradictions of life, he had groped for solace that October day in the pre-dawn darkness of his beloved woodlands. And searching for the first glimmer of the new morning, he cried out, "Oh, Mr. Creator, why did You make this universe?"

Softly he went on with the story: "And the Creator

answered me. 'You want to know too much for that little mind of yours,' He said. 'Ask me something more your size.'

"So I said, 'Dear Mr. Creator, tell me what man was made for.'

"Again He spoke to me, and He said, 'Little man, you are still asking for more than you can handle. Cut down the extent of your request and improve the intent.' "

The audience of 1000 boys and girls in the Macalester chapel sat absolutely still. Not a freshman fidgeted or coughed, but all leaned expectantly toward the feeble old man with the magically musical voice. He was bathed in a cone of light, the eternal flower standing plain in his lapel, and the love of God shining even more plainly in his eyes. He stood motionless on the platform, his seamed old man's face uplifted and rapt with the remembering.

"And then I asked my last question. 'Mr. Creator, why did You make the peanut?'

" 'That's better!' the Lord said, and He gave me a handful of peanuts and went with me back to the laboratory and, together, we got down to work."

He pulled on a flour-sack apron and shelled his handful of peanuts, grinding them to fine powder. This he heated, then squeezed the mass under a hand press until its oils flowed freely and he had collected a cupful. He studied it long and hard, subjected it to a whole battery of heat and temperature tests, and was heartened by the results. Unlike particles of animal fat, each of which was imprisoned inside a gelatinous membrane, peanut oil would blend with other substances in emulsion and could easily be broken down to margarine, soap, cooking and rubbing oils—even cosmetics!

Exhilarated, he turned to the cake of meal, added water, heated and stirred it, sometimes tasting it and adding a pinch of sugar or salt. When it had cooled and looked like a pitcher of creamy milk, he filled a glass and drank it off. "It *is* milk!" he said aloud, and grinned back at himself in a chipped looking glass. And it *was* milk, not produced by any cow, but abundant in precisely the same food values. And a mere handful of peanuts made a whole glassful!

Now the hours fled, the whole day and the night, as he literally tore the peanut apart, isolating its fats and gums and resins and sugars and starches. Spread before him were pentoses, pentosans, legumins, lysin, amido and amino acids, all chemically pried from the remarkable little bundle of vegetable energy called the peanut. Endlessly he tested different combinations under varying degrees of heat and pressures and, miraculously, his hoard of synthetic treasures grew: candy and peanut butter and flour; ink, dyes, shoe polish, creosote, salve and shaving cream. From the red skin of the nut he fabricated a paper finer than linen. From the hulls he made a soil conditioner, insulating board and fuel briquettes; binding another batch with adhesive, he pressed it, buffed it to a high gloss—and held in his hands a light and weatherproof square that looked precisely like marble and was every bit as hard.

All through the daylight and darkness he worked, and for another day and another night, huddled over his single lamp in the surrounding gloom, dismissing the worried students who tapped at his door—"Are you

all right, Dr. Carver?"—with a curt, "Yes! Yes! Please
let me be." He left the laboratory only to fetch more
peanuts and occasionally, absent-mindedly, threw some
in his mouth for nourishment.

But the truth was that now his strength came from
within. He felt himself to be in God's hands, the mortal
instrument of a divine revelation. Later he would say,
"The great Creator gave us three kingdoms, the animal,
the vegetable and the mineral. Now he has added a
fourth—the kingdom of synthetics." And years afterward, when the new science of chemurgy had been
defined as an attempt to create wealth from the dormant
power of the soil and air and sun, when Henry Ford
would proclaim that "I foresee the time when industry
shall no longer denude the forests but shall draw its
materials largely from the annual products of the fields,"
then men would say that Carver had been a chemurgist
before chemurgy was a word, and Christy Borth would
write of the peanut man's long ago experiments:

"Here was the transmutation of waste into wealth.
He made paper from the Southern pine—and 25 years
later his process led to a major new industry. He
made synthetic marble from peanut hulls and wood
wastes—and his efforts presaged the fabrication of plastics of all sorts from vegetable matter. Substituting
cellulose for steel, automobile-makers would soon be
building 350 pounds of agricultural products into every
car."

So it was that infinitely more important even than
the things Carver made was the stunning truth that he
was among the first to see and open out for all the future
generations—that in everything that grew was locked
the chemical magic that men could forge to their use,

not for food alone, but perhaps for all of their earthly needs.

Years later, Secretary of Agriculture Orville L. Freeman would laud Carver as a seer, as well as a doer: "His vision built opportunities and new industries out of the soil, and he inspired researchers to look for buried treasures in farm commodities."

Today more than 1000 Department of Agriculture scientists in four main laboratories and ten field stations are doing the work that Carver, alone and unaided, pioneered: studying farm products and how they can be taken apart, modified and remade into new products. And over the past three decades as much as 13 percent of America's farm output has gone into industrial production.

Carver looked forward to the day when the South would realize what a vast storehouse it had in its farms. "His dream," says Secretary Freeman, "is being fulfilled today on an even broader scale than he projected."

None of these lofty considerations even occurred to George Carver on that October night in 1915 when he finally sagged back on his workbench, gray and trembling with fatigue. He knew only that with God's guidance he had made it so that men could use every peanut harvested throughout the land, and that if the peanut crop doubled, trebled!—as it was to do in a scant four years—then still every farmer would find a ready buyer in the marketplace. And wearily he stumbled to his feet and walked out into the chill sunrise to offer his devout thanks.

In the years ahead, he kept adding to the remarkable roll of products made from the little peanut. By the time he died there were well over 300, and scores of factories had been built to make them, and their range staggered the mind: mayonnaise, instant coffee, cheese, chili sauce, shampoo, bleach, axle grease, linoleum, metal polish, wood stains, adhesives, plastics and wallboard. The peanut, Carver had shown, could provide virtually everything man needed to sustain life.

By 1919, once-destitute Coffee County was prospering as never before. Suddenly it was the wealthiest section in all Alabama, and the people jubilantly raised $3000 for a stone memorial to commemorate forever the ravening beetle that had dragged them to despair. Why? Because it was the boll weevil's very destructiveness— and the endless supplications of "the Tuskegee man"— that had freed them at last from the iron bondage of King Cotton.

Now Enterprise had a new $25,000 shelling plant, and a few years later the surrounding area was producing more peanuts than had ever been grown in any like-sized stretch of land in the world. And what could be done in the countryside around Enterprise, Alabama, could be done—and was—all around Albany, Georgia; and Elizabeth City, North Carolina; and Suffolk, Virginia. Everywhere across the South the once-despised goober began putting fresh life into the tortured soil and hard cash into the pockets of near-desperate farmers.

And steadily the harvest grew. At the century's turn, the dollar value of America's total peanut crop—which came to less than 100 million pounds—was so insignificant that it is not recorded. Today it is our sixth most important agricultural product. The two billion pounds harvested from six million acres are worth close to $300 million to the farmer and another $200 million to business and industry. Across the United States, peanuts are now a national institution, as familiar as ice cream and hot dogs. In Africa, Asia and South America, they have become a vital source of food. And still their possibilities in commerce and science are far from exhausted. Medical researchers have recently found something in the peanut that seems to stem the heretofore uncontrollable bleeding of hemophiliacs. Experiments are being conducted toward the day when astronauts may grow peanuts in their rocket ships, for the plant needs little room, gives off vital oxygen, and four cupfuls of nuts provides more than enough calories for a man's daily diet.

And all this beginning with an aging teacher of agriculture, who could not believe that God would have called his attention to the insignificant peanut without some high purpose.

Meanwhile Carver's renown was spreading beyond the confines of Tuskegee, beyond the borders of Alabama. More and more he was invited to address farm and school groups on the new agricultural revolution— although at least one such scheduled talk had to be canceled when the local newspaper whined that it would be presumptuous for a Negro to lecture white students on *any* subject. To most people, though, black and white, the color of Carver's skin meant far less than the fact that he was forever ready to advise them on a sweeping array of problems. His door stood open to all who could come to see him, and he spent hours each day answering the letters of those who couldn't. Soon so much mail was pouring in on him—much of it addressed simply to "The Peanut Man"—that a sub-station of the Tuskegee post office had to be established at the Institute.

"What's wrong with my dirt?" wrote one man. "It grows everything poor. Here's a sample." And Carver would dutifully shake out the envelope full of soil, analyze it and recommend the needed nutrients.

Wrote someone else: "My corn's stunted and my woman says she's taking the kids back to her ma if I don't paint the house. Please advise." Back went Carver's counsel: the corn field ought to be left fallow for a year, but if that was not possible, a hybrid seed would improve the stand; and a few hours' labor with a color wash from local clay would keep the family intact.

Many people sent money with their questions, all of which was returned with the answers. From a group of wealthy peanut planters in Florida came a check for $100 and a box of badly diseased specimens. If Carver could tell them how to cure their crop, they promised to put him on a monthly retainer at the same amount. Carver quickly recognized the problem as a lime deficiency, and so wrote to the growers, sending their check back with his reply. "As the good Lord charged nothing to grow your peanuts," he concluded, "I do not think it would be fitting of me to charge anything for curing them."

God was ever part of his sense and sum of things, ever his motivating force. When a young visitor from the North saw the stacks of mail on his desk, he kindly said, "You are surely making a great contribution to your race, Professor."

To which Carver replied, "My son, I am only God's helper in this work. And I am certain He has not had in mind any particular race, but the needs of all humanity."

Among the substantial new business enterprises built on the burgeoning peanut harvest was one launched by

Mr. Tom Huston of Columbus, Georgia. Before long little cellophane bags filled with "Tom's Toasted Peanuts" were being trucked throughout the South and the company had a standing offer to buy all the peanuts brought to their plant. "There's a check and a cheerful signer waiting right at the scales," they notified every farmer within 100 miles. But when Mr. Huston sought to broaden his line of products by manufacturing peanut butter, he ran into trouble—the oil kept settling out of the paste, which then turned rancid. Off to Tuskegee he sent his chief chemist, Wade Moss.

Carver pondered the problem—and presently came up with a simple additive that held the peanut oil in perfect emulsion. Not long after, he helped Moss perfect a technique for coating peanuts with chocolate, and these were added to a growing list of Huston staples. Horrified to learn that the company was throwing away hundreds of pounds of peanut hulls every week, Carver showed them how to convert the waste into valuable soil conditioner and sawdust. Now Tom Huston himself came to Tuskegee—bearing a handsome sealskin blanket as a token of his great gratitude; Carver put it in the bottom of a trunk and, to the best of anyone's knowledge, never again took it out—and the Southern industrialist and the colored teacher spent hours in earnest conversation. As always Carver was a fountainhead of ideas about uses to which the peanut could be put, and had countless suggestions for saving labor and money in its preparation. At one point, in a burst of enthusiasm, Huston cried out, "My God, Carver, you've got to come to Columbus and work for me!"

And Carver smiled his gentle smile and said, "He isn't only *your* God, Mr. Huston. You can't expect Him to

devote Himself exclusively to the problems of Tom's
Toasted Peanuts—and you can't really expect it of me,
either. I'll help you all I can, but my place is here."

His help was of substantial proportions, and continued
over a 15-year period. Huston came to see him as often
as once a month and kept trying to press gifts on him.
Once he said, "Isn't there *anything* I can give you?
What do you want most of all?"

Carver's brow furrowed in thought and, unaccount-
ably, he said, "I'd like to have a diamond."

"It's yours!" Huston promptly declared, and barely a
week later the diamond, mounted in a rich platinum
ring, was delivered to Carver at the Institute. On his
next visit, understandably expectant, Huston asked
whether the professor liked the gift. Yes, yes, was the
reply. It was just fine.

"Well—uh—why aren't you wearing it?"

"Wearing it?" said Carver, surprised that anyone could
have misunderstood. "Why, I never meant to wear it."
Whereupon he led Huston to his geological specimen
case and lifted the lid. There lay the diamond, rounding
out his collection of rare minerals.

But Huston was to have the last word. In 1931 he
commissioned a sculptor to design a bronze likeness of
Carver's head. It was presented to the Institute at the
commencement exercises, an occasion somewhat damp-
ened for Carver because the rest of the faculty made
him wear the traditional cap and gown. The plaque is
now a focal point of the Carver Museum at Tuskegee.

By the end of World War I the infant peanut industry
was worth $80 million and the prospects were heady.
Eager to capitalize on this unexpected abundance, and

to preserve and expand it, Southern planters banded together and in 1919, organized themselves as the United Peanut Associations of America. Their aims were two-fold: to advertise and otherwise promote an ever-growing use of their products; and to somehow win for themselves a measure of protection against a sudden flood of peanuts from the Orient. Chinese planters and Japanese processors, quick to seize commercial opportunity, were shipping some 30 million bushels of peanuts a year to the newly-developed American market, fully half of what could reasonably be absorbed. Using coolie labor and paying an import duty of less than a penny a pound, Far Eastern producers could conceivably squeeze American farmers right out of the peanut business.

The planters scheduled a meeting in Montgomery for September 13, 1920, and agreed—after emotional debate —to have Carver come and tell them about some of the things he had done with the peanut. "If we need a nigger to tell us how to run our business then I say we're in the wrong business," shouted a onetime Georgia red-neck, only recently elevated from direst poverty by the peanut.

More enlightened views prevailed. Carver, it was pointed out, had virtually created their business. He knew more about the peanut and its potential than any living human and so the invitation was duly sent off to Tuskegee and early on Tuesday, September 14, Carver stepped down from the train in Montgomery and asked the way to the Exchange Hotel. In that very building, nearly 60 years before, the Confederate Congress had voted to instruct General Beauregard to open fire on Fort Sumter.

It was a brutally hot day. A glaring sun beat down on

Carver as he walked along Jefferson Davis Avenue, his shoulders bent and his arms pulled taut by the weight of the two cardboard suitcases he carried, each one heavily packed with dozens of specimen bottles. At the hotel he found that the peanut men had gone over to City Hall. He turned back downtown, his alpaca coat dark with perspiration. Inquiries at City Hall led him from one office to another until, when he finally found out where the Peanut Associations had been, it was too late: they had already returned to the hotel. Again he picked up the heavy cases and again went out into the searing heat. By now it was nearly midday.

At the hotel, the doorman refused to let him in. "Sorry, old uncle," he said amiably. "There's no colored allowed in here."

Carver set his cases down on the sidewalk, trembling with fatigue and frustration. There was no point in arguing, he knew. Still, it took him some little time to remember his own axiom, that flinging hatred back at ignorance was an exercise in uselessness and sterility. Finally he said, "My name is Carver and I am expected at the United Peanut Associations meeting. Would you be kind enough to tell them I am waiting here?"

There followed a whispered conversation between the doorman and a bellboy—complete with some snickering and frankly incredulous glances at the sad old figure and his battered suitcases—but the bellboy eventually went inside and, after a time, returned to lead Carver around to a service elevator. Just outside the meeting room, he was stopped again and told that the peanut men were starting their luncheon. He would have to wait.

Years afterward, recalling this moment, Carver said that it would have been easy for him to simply pick up his cases and leave. "I am human and this is what every instinct urged me to do. But as I stood in the hallway with people pushing by me as though I didn't exist, God reminded me that I had not come all the way to Montgomery to indulge my personal feelings. Nor had I come to contribute to the wealth of the businessmen and big planters in that meeting room. I had come to help the thousands of sandy-land farmers I had persuaded to get into peanuts in the first place, and this organization was their instrument, too."

It was nearly 2 P.M. before Carver was introduced to the suddenly stiffly-silent assemblage. There wasn't a hint of resentment in his manner as he opened his suitcases and, long-accustomed to the chill of white audiences, tried to establish contact with a few little jokes. "Your Montgomery heat is hard on people," he said lightly, "but I hope you won't complain as it is excellent for peanuts." A few small smiles broke out in the swarm of impassive faces before him and he addressed himself directly to them, and soon could feel all the rest listening raptly, his message transcending their innate hostility.

As well it might! For he had brought them nothing less than the guidelines to lasting prosperity. Here in the bottles he held aloft for their edification were stains made from peanuts, tan and russet for leather, black and green and blue for wood. Here was soap, shaving lotion and face powder; here candy and condiments and milk products ranging from ice cream to cheese. He told them that while 100 pounds of cows' milk made ten pounds of cheese, the same amount of peanut milk made more than twice that much. There was no end of useful things that could be done with the funny-looking little goober, he said, and therefore no limit to the market.

By now the planters were wide-eyed and hanging on his words, and when he ended by telling them that the peanut was meant to be a blessing to all men, and that its future depended on their imagination and efforts, they burst into clattering applause. Many crowded forward to inspect the exhibits, muttering their amazement— "It's so hard to believe . . . all that from peanuts!"— and some even thought to thank Carver for his presentation. When at last order had been restored, Alabama Congressman Henry B. Steagall took the floor:

"Following the speaker who has just addressed this meeting I certainly would feel greatly embarrassed if I attempted to talk about peanuts in a way to instruct anybody. No man who has heard this address here today could stand in the face of the argument that here is an industry that touches the necessities of life throughout every nook and cranny of the nation. Certainly here is an infant industry that could plead a case of protection for itself. And when the time comes that this question must be thrashed out before the American Congress, I propose to see that Professor Carver is there in order that he may instruct them a little about peanuts, as he has done here on this occasion."

There was more applause, cries of "Hear! Hear!" The planters clapped each other on the back and excitedly voiced their determination to fight for recognition in the new tariff bill. In the tumult and confusion, only a few of them noticed when Carver put his bottles away, hefted his suitcases and went out. Scuffing along the hot and airless street as quickly as he could with his awkward burden, he just caught the 4 P.M. eastbound express.

But the peanut men had not forgotten him. Early in January they sent him an urgent telegram: "Want you in Washington morning of 20th. Depending on you to show Ways and Means Committee possibilities of the peanut." Carver wrote them that he would be there, then turned his attention back to his everyday duties.

The lady teachers, though, were all atwitter at the news. For days the dining hall buzzed as, again and again, they congratulated Carver on the great honor he had brought to the school and vied with each other in trying to imagine how it would be when *their* Professor Carver stood up before those Congressmen and had his say on—what was it again?—the tariff bill. Then they started to nag him about his clothes—his best suit was still the one his Iowa classmates had bought for him 28 winters before, and his favorite tie was a flowing four-in-hand knitted from dyed corn husks. "Surely you're not going to wear *that* to Washington," they clucked. "Surely you will buy a new suit."

Until, pushed to a corner by their gentle badgering, he finally exclaimed, "Now look here! If it's a new suit they want to see I can send them one in a box. But if it's me, why, I think they'll take me dressed as I am." And grinned at their consternation.

He arrived in Washington on Thursday, January 20, and went directly to the Committee hearings in the House of Representatives office building. The Peanut Associations officials were already on hand and much relieved to see him; advocates of a higher duty for walnuts and dates and poultry had presented their briefs, and the room rang with shout and acrimony, and the Congressmen were testy with the witnesses and each other—and the question of peanuts had not even been put on the docket yet. Carver listened for a while longer and then, to the absolute horror of the planters, left his cases in their care and said he would come back later.

Outside he found a cab and asked to be taken to the National Zoological Garden. Up Connecticut Avenue he rode, eyes sliding over monuments and memorials, but fixing sharply on every tree and patch of greenery they passed. At the Garden, he walked slowly and alone along Rock Creek, engrossed as always by the miracle of growth. He ran long fingers over unfamiliar shrubbery, whispering to himself, utterly content and caught up with nature's never-ending surprises. All thoughts of the tariff had fled from his mind and he was oblivious to the world and the works of men. When he came upon an unusual Chinese arborvitae whose bleak rust color betrayed a fungus, he fell to his knees in the damp winter earth, searching the underside of the bush until he had found what he was looking for. Then he hailed an attendant, pointed out the parasitic growth and explained that it must be treated promptly lest it spread to the other plantings.

"I'll report it," the man promised and, satisfied, Carver started back toward Connecticut Avenue and the hearings.

But the matter of peanuts was not brought before the Ways and Means Committee that day, nor all of the following morning. With plainly increasing boredom and irritability, the members heard arguments in favor of protection for rice and meat manufactures of all sorts. Spacious though it was, the hearing room grew stuffy

with smoke and tempers turned ragged as endless groups
fussed in debate and contended for the committee's favor. By mid-afternoon of Friday, the 21st, the Peanut
Associations people were hollow-cheeked and rigid with
nervous agony. "We'll be lucky to get half an hour,"
groaned one. "We're sunk!"

"Better tell Carver what to say," urged Congressman
Steagall.

"Ah, what's the use? It's too late."

It was past 4 P.M. when the first peanut spokesman was
called forward. Adjournment had been set for 5. "Gentlemen, I'll try to be brief," said the representative of the
Virginia-Carolina Co-operative Peanut Exchange.

"Please do!" said the weary Congressman from Texas,
John N. Garner.

"A protective tariff is the only thing that can save our
small Southern farmer from ruin. We're not asking for
any special advantage. We ask only an import duty that
would more nearly equal the difference between producing peanuts with cheap labor abroad and what it costs us
to do the job with our free American labor."

"That's all anybody's asking," said committee Chairman Joseph W. Fordney wryly. And despite the tension a
clang of laughter scattered through the room.

"We need a tariff of at least four cents a pound!" the
peanut man cried desperately.

"Yes, well we'll take it under advisement. Any other
witnesses?"

The clerk called the name of George W. Carver. Every
head snapped around, eyes gaping at the spectacle of
the gray-haired colored man in the time-worn suit, a sprig
of arborvitae in his lapel, lugging two heavy cases toward
the speaker's stand. Was this a mistake? Some kind of a

joke? In the sudden hush someone was heard to snigger, "Reckon if he gets enough peanuts to go with his watermelon he's a right happy coon."

Carver heard it clearly, but he had heard worse and didn't turn a hair. When he reached the stand and began unpacking his cases, Chairman Fordney said, "I think, considering the lateness of the hour, sir, that we can allow you only ten minutes."

Carver's heart sank. It would take him ten minutes just to gain the attention of these people, sprawled laxly in their chairs and driven to exhaustion and torpor by two days of harangues and an avalanche of dry statistics. He went on taking his bottles out, groping for a way to begin.

"What do you know about the tariff?" Mr. Garner called out.

"Not a thing. I came to talk about peanuts."

There was a titter of amusement. Some of the Congressmen sat up. Carver took a deep breath and said, "I have been asked to tell you something about the possibilities of the peanut and its extension. But we'll have to hurry if we are to extend it because in ten minutes you will tell me to stop."

More laughter, then a bewildering cross-current of questions, one drowning out another. The Congressmen began to shout at one another and, without having uttered another word, Carver was notified that three of his ten minutes were gone.

"Well, you took those three minutes so I supposed you would give them back to me."

The grumbling died down. Again they were watching him as he held up a clump of chocolate-covered peanuts. "You don't know how delicious this is," he said in the high, silvery voice, "so I will taste it for you." And he dropped the confection into his mouth. They laughed heartily and leaned toward him, all of them. He had their attention, at last. Now if he only had the time . . .

What followed is recorded in the Congressional Record, *Hearings Before the Committee on Ways and Means, House of Representatives, on Schedule G, Agricultural Products and Provisions, January 21, 1921:*

MR. CARVER. I am engaged in agricultural research work and have given some attention to the peanut. I can tell you that it is one of the very richest products of the soil, rich in food values, rich in properties of its chemical constituents, and wonderfully rich in properties for utilization. If I may have a little space to put these things down —thank you. Now I should like to exhibit them to you. I am going to just touch a few high places here and there because in ten minutes you will tell me to stop. These are a few of the products which we have developed from the peanut. This is a breakfast food containing peanut and sweet potato. It is wholesome, easily digested and delicious in flavor. The peanut and sweet potato are twin brothers. If all other food were destroyed, a person could live well on peanuts and sweet potatoes. They contain all nutriments necessary to man.

THE CHAIRMAN. What is that other stuff?

MR. CARVER. Here is ice cream powder made from the peanut. Simply mixed with water, it produces an unusually rich and delicious ice cream, not to be distinguished from ice cream made with pure cream. In these bottles are dyes extracted from the skin of peanuts. I have found 30 different dyes. They have been tested in the laboratory and found to hold their colors and to be

harmless to the skin. Here is a substitute for quinine. We
can hardly overestimate the medicinal properties of the
peanut. They are many and varied. These are various
kinds of food for livestock. You will find that cattle thrive
on them and the increase in milk is pronounced. I have
two dozen or so others, but I see my time is about up. I
should like to say that the soil and climate of the South
is particularly suited to the cultivation of peanuts and
that they could be produced in much greater quantities
if a larger market for them were developed. It would
seem a great pity if this crop were lost to us and our people forced to depend on foreign and inferior peanuts.
Thank you.

mr. garner. Mr. Chairman, all this is very interesting. I
think his time should be extended.

the chairman. Very well. Gentlemen, do you all agree?

voices. Yes, yes.

the chairman. Will you continue, Mr. Carver?

mr. carver. I shall be happy to do so, sir.

mr. rainey. Is the varied use of the peanut increasing?

mr. carver. Oh, yes. We are just beginning to know its
value.

mr. rainey. In that case, is it not going to be such a valuable product that the more we have of them here the better off we are?

mr. carver. Well, now, that depends. It depends upon
the problems that these other gentlemen have brought
before you.

MR. BARKLEY. Could we get too much of them, they being so valuable for stock food and everything else?

MR. CARVER. Well, of course we would have to have protection for them. That is, we could not allow other countries to come over and take over our rights.

MR. GARNER. I thought you said you didn't know anything about the tariff.

MR. CARVER. Well, I know it's what keeps the other fellow out of our business. (Laughter) I wish to say here in all sincerity that America produces better peanuts than any other part of the world, so far as I have been able to find out.

MR. RAINEY. Then we need not fear these inferior peanuts from abroad at all. They would not compete with our better peanuts.

MR. CARVER. Well, you know that's like everything else. You know some people like oleomargarine just as well as they do butter. So sometimes you have to protect a good thing.

MR. OLDFIELD. The dairy people did not ask for a tax on butter, but they did put a tax on oleomargarine.

MR. GARNER. And they did use the taxing power to put it out of business.

MR. CARVER. Oh, yes, yes, sir. That is all the tariff means —to put the other fellow out. (Laughter) Maybe— maybe I'd better stop.

THE CHAIRMAN. Go ahead, brother. Your time is unlimited.

MR. CARVER. Well, here is milk from peanuts.

MR. OLDFIELD. Don't you think we ought to put a tax on peanut milk so as to keep it from competing with the dairy products? (Laughter)

MR. CARVER. No, sir. It is not going to affect the dairy product. It has a distinct value all its own.

MR. BARKLEY. Why won't it replace the dairy product?

MR. CARVER. We do not now have as much milk and butter as we need in the United States.

MR. BARKLEY. How does it go in punch? (Laughter)

MR. CARVER. Well, I will give you some punches. (Laughter)

VOICES. Good! Attaboy! (Laughter)

MR. CARVER. Here is one with orange, here one with lemon, and this one with cherry. Here is instant coffee which already has in it cream and sugar. Here is the preparation for making regular coffee. Here is buttermilk, Worcestershire sauce, pickles—all made from the peanut.

THE CHAIRMAN. Did you make all those products yourself?

MR. CARVER. Yes, sir. They are made in the research laboratory. That's what a research laboratory is for. The sweet potato products number 107 up to date.

MR. GARNER. What? I didn't catch that last statement.

MR. CARVER. Yes, indeed—I said 107. From sweet potatoes we have made ink, relishes, pomade, mucilage, to mention only a few things. But I must stick to peanuts. (Laughter) The peanut will beat the sweet potato by far. I have barely begun on it. Here are mock oysters which would fool most of you. I have developed recipes for mock meat dishes from peanuts. They are delicious. We are going to use less and less meat as science develops the products of nature.

MR. RAINEY. So you're going to ruin the livestock business. (Laughter)

MR. CARVER. Oh, no. But peanuts can be eaten when meat can't. Peanuts are the perfect food. They are always safe.

MR. BARKLEY. Where did you learn all this?

MR. CARVER. From a book.

MR. BARKLEY. What book?

MR. CARVER. The Bible. It says that God has given us everything for our use. He has revealed to me some of the wonders of this fruit of His earth. In the first chapter of Genesis we are told, "Behold, I have given you every herb that bears seed upon the face of the earth, and every tree bearing seed. To you it shall be meat." That's what He means about it—meat. There is everything there to strengthen, nourish and keep the body alive and healthy.

MR. CAREW. Mr. Carver, where did you go to school?

MR. CARVER. The last school I attended was the Agricultural College of Iowa. You doubtless remember Mr. Wilson who served in the cabinet here so long, Secretary of Agriculture James Wilson. He was my teacher for six years.

THE CHAIRMAN. What research laboratory do you work in now?

MR. CARVER. I am at Tuskegee Institute, Tuskegee, Alabama.

THE CHAIRMAN. Please go on.

He did. For nearly two hours he held the committee spellbound with his display of peanut products—vanishing cream, rubbing oils, dyes, stains, milk flakes—interspersing all the while his homilies and puckish humor. When he was finished, Mr. Carew said, "You have rendered this committee a great service." At Mr. Garner's suggestion, every member rose and applauded vigorously, and someone called out, "Come again—and bring your other products with you!" And the record shows that Chairman Fordney complimented the witness on the way he had handled his subject.

As Carver was leaving the hearing room, Congressman Alben W. Barkley of Kentucky stopped him and asked if he would submit a brief. "The testimony goes to the printer tonight, but I'll hold him up if you can send us your material. We'd like to have that."

Carver said that he would. On the train going back to Tuskegee, he wrote out a statement summarizing what he had told the committee, ending with, "I have nothing to sell. I manufacture nothing. And I feel sure you gentlemen will guard and put proper restrictions upon every interest that arises in harmful competition with ours without any suggestions of mine."

But the fact was that his presentation had been an infinitely more persuasive argument than all the facts, figures and supplications offered by the Peanut Associations. And so it was that the following year, when Congress passed the Fordney-McCumber tariff bill, domestic peanuts were covered by a duty of three cents a pound on all unshelled imports and four cents a pound on the shelled. And for a long time afterward, Congressman Steagall, recounting the story of Carver's testimony, would always conclude, "And to think I wanted them to tell him what to say!"

There seemed to be no end to the astonishing catalogue of things Carver could do with a handful of peanuts. He developed a peanut flour, four times richer in protein and with eight times as much fat as wheat flour, whose minimal carbohydrate content made it a valuable substitute in diabetic diets. Pulverized and packaged, peanut shells began to be used by gardeners who had always depended on imported—and expensive—peat moss to tone up clayey earth. The results were gratifying: the crushed shells held more moisture and, in the bargain, fed nitrogen, phosphate and potash to the soil.

Once, returning from an exhausting speaking tour with a cold and the racking cough that had plagued him off and on through his life, Carver shut himself up in his laboratory and, hours later, emerged with a remedy. He started with creosote, whose therapeutic value in respiratory ailments had long been known, but whose use was severely restricted by a taste so vile that only the most resolute patient could stomach it. Working it into a stable emulsion with peanut oil, Carver devised a medicine that, in the same tasteful dose, provided the patient with nourishing food values, as well. It promptly cured his cough.

Not long after, the Sharp and Dohme laboratories,

learning of the new tonic, sought to manufacture it commercially under the trade name of Penol. Carver had no objection to this—not that it much mattered since, as usual, he had obtained no patent on his latest discovery. But though he agreed to supervise its preparation, he refused absolutely to permit the use of his name in exploiting the new product and, with the onset of the Great Depression, it was abandoned. It remained a standard remedy at the Institute, though, and anyone with a cough or cold had only to knock on Dr. Carver's door and he would hand out a small bottle of the peanut oil-and-creosote mixture with his blessing.

The women in town had been delighted with the face cream Carver gave them. It had a silky texture and its peanut oil base seemed unusually effective against skin blemishes of all sorts. Soon, though, many were reluctantly returning it: it made their faces fleshy and fat, they reported. Carver pondered this for some time, then concluded that anything so enriching to facial muscles ought to have the same effect on all muscles. Wouldn't peanut oil, then, make a more potent base for rubbing compounds than those made from mineral or cottonseed oil? Mightn't it nourish muscles atrophied by accident or disease? Mightn't it help Lonny Johnston?

Lonny was a familiar figure on the campus, a bright and cheerful lad of fourteen whose father tended the farm animals. Years before, a skittish horse had kicked Lonny in the leg, tearing some ligaments behind his knee. In healing, the ligaments had grown tight and the right leg stiffened into what appeared to be permanent lameness. Carver talked to the boy's parents, and one Saturday afternoon Lonny hiked up his trouser leg and stretched out on the laboratory table, apprehensive, but trusting implicitly in the Professor.

"I can't promise that this will do you any good," Carver said, "but it surely can't do any harm. Now if God is with us . . ."

He poured some of his peanut oil rubbing preparation into one hand and, with those marvelously supple fingers, began to massage the withered ligaments. For 20 minutes he worked away, calling up funny little stories out of his inexhaustible supply as he rubbed, so that Lonny was downright disappointed when the session ended.

"How does it feel?" Carver asked.

"Well—sort of *fresh.*"

"Good. Now you come back here every day as soon as school is out. We'll soon find out if the three of us can get that knee to bend properly again."

"The three of us?"

"You and I and the good Lord."

The peanut oil massages continued for half a year. In little more than two months Lonny was striding along with only the barest trace of a limp. Soon after he was playing baseball and, by the time he was graduated from high school, he had won varsity letters in three sports.

Meanwhile Carver had begun treating a youngster who had been stricken with poliomyelitis, then known as infantile paralysis. Again the results were heartening and, at a meeting of the newly-formed National Chemurgic Council in Dearborn, Michigan, Carver showed photographs of the boy's leg as he progressed from crutches to a cane to vigorous and unimpeded activity.

Somehow the Associated Press picked up the story and soon the news had been flashed across the country that the peanut man had invented a miraculous cure for infantile paralysis.

Carver went to great pains to deny that his treatment was in any sense a cure. He pointed out that neither massage nor ointment of any kind could have an effect on the disease itself. At best, such therapy might temper the devastating aftereffects by restoring a measure of life to lame and wasted limbs. But it was like trying to stem an avalanche by commanding it to turn back. Carver's protests were drowned in a clamor of flaring hopes that would not be repressed. As it happened, a vicious epidemic of polio had swept the United States that summer of 1932, and now a pathetic parade of crippled children were brought to Tuskegee by mothers and fathers whose eyes, more beseeching than any words, begged for help. They came from every part of the South, and from as far away as New York and California, and their cars lined the narrow street in front of Carver's laboratory the day-long. He saw as many as he humanly could, sometimes rubbing away until every other window on the campus had gone dark, and from early morning until 10 or 11 P.M. on Saturday and Sunday.

His mail swelled to an incredible 1500 letters a month. He was besieged by endless telegrams and long distance telephone calls, all from people who pleaded for a bottle of his magic elixir, offering sometimes staggering sums of money in return. A factory could not have filled the demand, nor could Carver have ever brought himself to take anything from the unfortunate men and women imploring his help. All he could tell them was that his "cure" was nothing but peanut oil, and that they could buy a whole half-gallon of it at the corner grocery store for about 85 cents.

There were inevitable misunderstandings, even bitterness. After a talk once, a lady asked Carver whether he believed the sufferers who came to him benefited more from his oil or from prayer. He replied that prayer came before all things. Why, then, she persisted, didn't he advise these people to quit the use of *all* medicines and oils, to put themselves wholly in God's hands?

"My dear Madam," he said, "how can any of us deny the reality around us? The most valuable things in life are God's handiwork expressed in nature. Why else would He have put the herbs and the healing ointments of the fields onto this earth if He didn't mean for us to use them?"

One Saturday a man pushed roughly past the patiently-waiting people and burst into the laboratory. Ignoring the child on whom Carver was working, he announced, "I got this bad leg. I want you to fix it."

Carver said that he could not and turned back to the child.

The man's face turned stormy red and he seized the frail scientist by the arm, spinning him around. "Don't you turn your back on me, nigger!" he cried out. "I drove 100 miles to get my leg fixed and now you tell me you can't—well you better have a damn good reason!"

Carver detested this kind of scene. Had he been anywhere else, he would have just walked off. Now, though, hands trembling but his voice firm with purpose, he said, "Neither my prayers nor the power of this medicine could possibly penetrate the profanity in your heart. I

can't help you because you would rather hate me than
be helped. Do you understand?"

The man said nothing. For long and tense moments
he glared at Carver. Then, still without speaking, he
turned and stomped out.

Despite Carver's caution in making any claims for his
peanut oil, the results he obtained with it were striking.
Records kept on the 250 cases he treated show that in
every instance there was at least some improvement, and
many patients recovered completely. His work began to
receive serious scientific attention. In 1939, the National
Foundation for Infantile Paralysis made a substantial
grant to Tuskegee for the purpose of setting up a polio
treatment and study center, an especially valuable contribution since colored children could not be accepted at
the nation's other major polio clinic in Warm Springs,
Georgia. Further endowments were made by the Rockefeller Foundation, and when it became clear that the
aging Carver could not possibly cope with what had
become a rigorous full-time job, a highly-skilled ortho-
pedist, Dr. John W. Chennault, was named director of
the Tuskegee Polio Center. But Carver's methods remained at the heart of the treatment.

Did the peanut oil, then, actually exercise some inexplicable curative power on paralyzed muscles? Carver
himself was never certain, although he did feel that the
human skin could more easily absorb peanut oil than
any other kind. The fact was that his own uncanny gift
in the use of massage—learned so long ago as a "rubber"
for the athletic teams at Ames, Iowa, and never forgotten—probably contributed more to the healing process than anything else. Said Dr. Chennault recently: "He
had a genius for the care of muscular injury, an over-

whelming knowledge of the anatomy. He could run his fingers over an afflicted leg and say, 'Life ends about here,' setting out a paralyzed muscle and then going to work on it with more competence than I have seen in the most professionally-trained physical therapists."

Of course Carver was greatly gratified by the long-lasting good the little peanut, in all its myriad forms, had brought to so many different people. But it seems safe to say that one of its blessings, most movingly chronicled after his death, would have touched a very special corner of his heart. A week or so after the weary old man had been laid to rest, his young assistant, Austin W. Curtis, Jr., received this letter from a missionary in the Belgian Congo:

"I write to express to you our great sense of loss at the news of Dr. Carver's passing. We have been so indebted to him for 25 years, when I first learned of his work in extracting milk from the peanut. You see, it has never been possible for us to keep farm animals in interior Africa, for they are attacked by tigers and sickened by tsetse flies. So it used to be that when a new mother could give no milk her baby soon died. When I wrote this information to Dr. Carver in 1918, he responded by instructing us on the culture of the peanut plant and with detailed information on the procedure for deriving milk from the nuts. Hundreds of infants were so saved from death, and for this we can never properly express our thanks. But in this sad moment, let me try. Let me speak the gratitude of all of our people who live because of him to all of you who were graced by having known him. The world has lost a sainted human, but no man has ever more earned his heavenly rest."

VIII. The Sands of Time

IN THE SAME HALF HOUR HE ANSWERED
A LETTER FROM HENRY FORD, SHOWED
THE COOK HOW TO FRY BACON SO IT
WOULDN'T CURL AND HELPED MRS. WAG-
GENER WITH HER CROCHETING. THEN HE
HANDED ME ONE OF HIS OLD PAYCHECKS
AND SAID, "GO ON, TAKE IT! OPPORTUNITY
WON'T WAIT—AND THE TRAIN LEAVES
AT 5 O'CLOCK."

—*L.A. Locklair*

Eᴀʀʟʏ ɪɴ July 1908, Carver set out on a trip to Missouri. He spent a reflective hour at his brother Jim's grave, and stayed the night with Aunt Mariah Watkins, who still lived in the little cabin by the schoolhouse. But he especially wanted to see Moses Carver. The rugged farmer of Carver's memory was now ninety-six years old, alone, enfeebled and plainly looking toward the time when he and the long-dead Susan would again be together. He was greatly moved by Carver's visit and talked animatedly for a while. But soon his attention seemed to lag and reluctantly, sadly, Carver got up to go.

"When you left here that day," Moses Carver suddenly said, "walking down that road, such a skinny little shaver, Aunt Sue allowed as how you'd come back home by dark."

"I almost did," Carver said, smiling, remembering.
"No, no. She was just speaking out what we both
wished for. But I told her you had a powerful long way
to travel, and that you weren't the turning-back kind."
He drew a deep, rheumy breath. "I'm proud you got
where you were going, George."

Carver ached with feeling and was unable to speak.
And after another long pause, the old man said, "Go on
up to your mother's cabin. You'll find her spinning wheel
there—I want you to have it."

It was a final farewell. Carver never saw any of the
old folks again, but Mary's spinning wheel would always
stand in a corner of his crowded room, and he never
passed it without running his fingers over the wood,
worn smooth and shining with the years, and it stirred
to a fresh memory the people and the land of his youth
and young manhood.

A few years before, he had moved into Rockefeller
Hall, a new boy's dormitory. And though he now had perhaps twice as much space, the new quarters seemed fully
as cluttered as had the old. Display cases were filled with
his collections of rocks and insects and fossils. Books
lined the wall and scientific journals stood in teetering
stacks on the desk and floor. His crocheting overflowed a
glass-covered table and his paintings were banked in
every odd corner—he almost never hung any—and,
throughout, a lavish, bewildering array of potted plants
and flower slips might persuade a stranger that he had
wandered into a hothouse.

Strangers came, and friends of every station and age.
Farmers sought him out with their questions about seed
and fertilizer and how best to decontaminate a well.
Townfolk asked about their gardens, and the boys in

the dormitory thought nothing of bringing him their homework—and Carver thought nothing of putting aside an experiment to puzzle with them over a problem in mathematics or animal husbandry. An endless procession of faculty children trooped to his door carrying strange rocks and dead birds and injured dogs, for there was, they said, nothing Professor Carver didn't know or couldn't do. When young Ernest Washington's pet goose suddenly sickened and died, he put it in a box for the walk over to Rockefeller Hall.

"But it's too late," Dr. Washington gently told his son. "The goose is dead."

"That doesn't matter," the boy replied with absolute confidence. "Professor Carver will make him better anyhow."

Washington came, too, and often, and sometimes in the middle of the night. Pressed and burdened beyond belief and unable to find rest, he would knock on Carver's door and apologetically say, "I thought perhaps you would like to walk a while." And Carver would dress and hurry out to join the principal, for he well knew the weight of worry and the nagging, numberless cares that Washington alone must carry. Nor did they often discuss the problems of the moment. Rather they walked along through the dark, talking of small things—and sometimes not talking at all—until perhaps an hour later, perhaps two or three, Washington was calmed and tired enough to seek sleep, and he would thank his friend and bid him goodnight.

Once someone scolded Carver for submitting to the annoyance of being wakened at one or two in the morning. "It is no annoyance," he replied, "but a privilege. Whenever Dr. Washington wants me I shall be ready."

It would be hard to find two more different men. Washington was now world-famous, outgoing, vigorous in speech and action, the acknowledged spokesman of his people. He had dined with President Theodore Roosevelt at the White House—exciting a storm of Southern protests, and even threats against his life—and struggled ceaselessly to enlist men of influence in the crusade for broadened Negro opportunity.

But Carver still found his deepest fulfillment in solitude, working in his laboratory or greeting the new dawn from a stump in his precious woodland. Though far from unmindful of an inexorable obligation to his race, he sought to meet it by reaching "the man farthest down" and lending him a hand up. Nor did he believe that the winning over of government officials and white businessmen was unimportant—it was only that he felt himself to be no good at it. And when, after Washington's death, he assumed the leadership of his people, he did it with trepidation and not a little reluctance.

And yet, deep within their beings, both men, sprung from the same roots of slavery, believed in the same essentials and labored toward a common goal. Both had a mystical feeling for the land and had never been afraid to sink their hands into it. Both had staked their trust in the ultimate power of education. And Washington, reflecting bitter personal experience, pointedly described their shared appraisal of the racial question when, in *The Story of the Negro,* he wrote:

Any black man willing to curse or abuse the white man easily gained for himself a reputation for great courage. He might spend but thirty minutes or an hour once a year in that kind of "vindication" of his race, but he got the reputation of being an exceedingly brave man. Another man who worked patiently and persistently for years in a Negro school, depriving himself of many of the comforts and necessities of life, in order to perform a service which would uplift his race, was likely to be denounced as a coward by these "heroes," because he chose to do his work without cursing.

In mid-October 1915, Washington left for still another speaking tour in the North. Carver talked with him on the morning of his departure—they discussed an exhibit the agriculture department was readying for the state fair—and was suddenly aware that the principal was gray with fatigue, and that his shoulders sagged as he waved good-bye and turned down the steps of the dining hall. It was the last time Carver would see him alive.

On the evening of October 25th, Washington spoke in New Haven—his subject was race tolerance—and, almost immediately afterward, fell ill. Still he insisted on going on to New York. But there were to be no more speeches for that valiant pilgrim. Days later, he collapsed and was rushed to a hospital, where doctors told him he might live only a few hours. Gasping for voice, Washington spoke to his friend, Robert Russa Moton, who was to succeed him as president of Tuskegee: "Take me home. I was born in the South. I have lived and labored in the South, and I wish to die and be buried in the South."

He was carried to the train and returned, the sad news having preceded him, to a great and solemn hush pervading the campus and reaching into every dormitory.

And early on the morning of November 14th, he died and was buried on a little rise of ground at the school. There was sorrow and a shattering sense of bereavement throughout the land. Millions of Negroes had learned to look to Washington for inspiration and what little hope they had, and now they could not conceive of the world without that heroic figure in it. Almost 100,000 of them contributed to a fund for a monument to his memory. Theodore Roosevelt came to Tuskegee for the funeral.

But more than most men, Carver felt Washington's death with the stunning shock of personal loss. They had had their disagreements and even during their walks in the dead of night it had always been "Dr. Washington" and "Professor Carver." But they had understood one another. They had been friends. And sensing that it would now be demanded of him, Carver felt unready to take his friend's place as a leader of their people. He was grateful to Roosevelt, who drew him aside after the final rites and said, "There is no more important work than what you are doing." And with work he sought to fill the incalculable void.

The memorial to Washington was completed the following year. It stands opposite the entrance to the Institute, a noble figure of the principal lifting a veil of ignorance from before the eyes of a frightened but eager boy, gently urging him forward into the new era. But the fact is that Tuskegee itself is Booker T. Washington's true memorial. The school he had brought to being 34 years before with a class of six in a tottering cabin now had 1500 boys and girls studying 38 trades and professions, and what someone called "the lengthened shadow of the man" would be felt in the nation for decades to come.

There were those on the faculty who thought Dr. Carver strange, as, indeed, by the lights of ordinary men, he was. His manner of dress grew ever more outlandish, coat and trousers usually having only venerability in common, and his cornhusk neckties flaunted the mismatched color—always garish—of whatever dye he happened to be testing. Even when he stopped on the campus to chat, he was forever stooping over to pick up a stone or weed, studying it, never in a hurry, but never quite idle. And if anyone asked about the usually obscure flower in his lapel with anything approaching real interest, Carver would reward him with a brisk little lecture on its morphology and neglected values. And 20 years after his death, he was most graphically remembered so, and any number of his old students and fellow-teachers could fondly mimic that tinkling voice saying, "Do you know what's inside this flower . . . ?"

Of course the single thing that made Carver seem strange to ordinary men was that he was not one of them. All of his attitudes and interests and aspirations were different. He had no ties, except to God, no obligations, except to his work. Granted the gift of genius, he guarded it zealously, so completely committed to whatever task he was at that his eyes saw almost everything else as trivia. And this particularly applied to the clothing he wore, the preoccupation of most people with financial gain, and the social amenities that fill so many lives. He had a wry wit and could be an engaging conversationalist, but no one could recall him ever attending any of the campus parties. Once, invited to a special dinner by one of the faculty members, he appeared with a note expressing appreciation for being asked, then turned to go.

"But—but aren't you coming in at all?" asked the perplexed teacher.

"Why, no," Carver said. "I must return to my work. But I did want to pay my respects."

Try as he might, Treasurer Logan could never get him to cash his paychecks with any regularity. Instead, he stuffed them inside little-used drawers, or between the pages of a book, or any other place where they could be filed and forgotten. When he did dig them out, most often it was to give them away. When the teachers were asked for contributions to a faculty center, Carver, horrified, emptied his pockets and said, "Why I seem to have only this dollar." Then, remembering, he plunged into a dresser drawer and flung out a year-old paycheck. "Here, this will help!" he called, and found another—"And this!"—and another—"And this!"—until the cache was empty and the astounded solicitor had a total of $625.

L.A. Locklair, now a successful mortician in Tuskegee, had helped Carver during his student days, digging and pulverizing clay for the color experiments, and delivering buckets of yellow paint to the railroad yard at Chehaw, where they were shipped to Birmingham and used on hundreds of boxcars. One summer the Institute had an opportunity to send some students north to work on the tobacco farms around Hartford, Connecticut. Young Locklair was eager to go for, like most of his classmates, he had to earn his keep. Unhappily, though, he did not have the $40 rail fare—until, again, Professor Carver

produced an old paycheck. "He promised to let me pay
it back in September," Locklair recently recalled, "but, of
course, when the time came he wouldn't take a penny.
In fact, he denied ever having lent me any money at all!"

There is no way of knowing the number of boys, white
as well as black, whose bills Carver paid in their times of
need. But virtually everyone who knew him remembers
at least one such instance—the frantic search through
the dresser drawer, the scribbled endorsements, the
thrust of a check or two into young hands, and the
brusque-with-embarrassment interruptions of all attempts at thanks. Others might toil and scramble and suffer for money, but Carver, who already possessed the
earth, had no use for it except as it might help others find
their way. Once he gave a student a dollar. "Let's see
what you can do with this," he said. The boy bought a
hen, a setting of eggs and a sack of feed. When he reported back to Carver some months later, he had over
$50 in cash and a flock of hens producing a steady in-
come. Nothing could have made his benefactor prouder.

In the end Carver had the last laugh—over what most
men would have considered a calamity. With the audi-
tors harrying Logan about the uncashed checks, he finally persuaded Carver to deposit them in the bank. And
there they had accumulated to a substantial sum when,
in February 1933, the bank was caught up in the great
national depression and failed. Carver was playing the
piano in Rockefeller Hall when the dismayed treasurer
came rushing to him with the news. He went right on
playing, remarking only, "I suppose that's what happens
when you hoard."

"Good Lord, man!" Logan cried out. "Don't you realize all your money is gone?"

Carver shrugged. "Well, wherever it's gone I guess they have more use for it than I did."

Still Logan felt a certain sense of responsibility for the professor's life-savings and prevailed on the bank to pay off 50 cents on the dollar. But when he reported this arrangement, Carver politely declined: "Give them my thanks, but tell them I deposited 100 cents on the dollar."

Back to the bank trudged the frustrated treasurer, to return with an offer of cotton in lieu of the cash—Carver could store it until prices went up again. But the answer was the same: "I didn't deposit cotton." At last he was induced to accept a small farm not far from the Institute, and eventually sold it to recoup at least part of his loss.

Carver's Bible class, which became the best-attended extracurricular activity on the campus, began quite by chance. Boys had taken to coming to his room in clusters of two and three on Sunday afternoons, and Carver would talk to them of the relationship between science and the Scriptures. With telling gestures and that piping voice, he acted out the roles of Biblical characters and, recounting the story of the Israelites in the Wilderness, actually showed them a variety of manna which he had somehow procured. He used fossil remains and mastodon teeth, hoarded from his Midwestern boyhood, to dramatize his lessons. And relating the wickedness of Sodom and Gomorrah, he climaxed his tale by suddenly touching off some chemicals in a great cloud of fume and flame. The boys leaped to their feet, gasping with shock and smoke—but never had religion seemed so close or real or important.

How could they *know* God? someone once asked. Would they ever *see* him?

"What are you studying?" Carver came back.

"Electricity."

"Have you ever seen electricity?"

"No, it's . . ."

"But when you make the proper contact, when you fulfill the laws of your trade, you can make a bulb light up, can't you, because the electricity is always *there*."

"Yes," the boy conceded.

"Well, God is always there, too—just waiting for you to make contact. He is all around you, in all the little things you look at but don't really see." He pulled the flower from his lapel and held it out. Every boy in the room hunched close. "God is here," Carver said. "The seed that made this flower was created millions of years ago. It survived drought and blizzards and the assaults of man himself. And in this flower is the beginning of a seed that will grow millions of years after all of us are gone."

Now he sank back in his chair, and they waited breathlessly, awed, eyes locked with his. And in a voice that rang with meaning, he said, "Can any of you believe that the miracle of this flower is no more than an accident?"

Week by week the group swelled until, unable any longer to squeeze into the crowded study, they moved out to the recreation room. When the proctors took to announcing the still-informal sessions just before Sunday dinner, Rockefeller Hall overflowed and the classes, now regularly scheduled, were shifted to the assembly room in the Carnegie Library. It was a rare week when all 300 seats were not filled.

Even when Carver was off on a lecture trip he almost always arranged his itinerary so that he would be back in Tuskegee by Sunday evening. And waiting, watch in hand, he began precisely on the stroke of six. He might start talking about the eternal laws of balance, the uncanny way nature had of evening things out. And soon, seemingly without relevance to either the laws of balance or the study of the Bible, he would be telling about this poor carpenter of long ago who had been struck by the unusual dryness of the season. He believed, Carver said, that in time there must inevitably be a long period of rain to fulfill nature's irrevocable law. But *why* did it not rain? Seeking guidance, he prayed to the Heavenly Father and the answer was given to him. Then, while others heedlessly went on with their everyday tasks and pleasures in the everlasting sunshine, the carpenter set to work building a boat. Night and day he labored, and men mocked him, for they lived far from the sea, until the laughter died in their throats. For at last the rains came, and it rained for 40 days and 40 nights, and across the land there was a great flood in divine retribution for those who had scorned God. And while the others were swept to their doom, the carpenter Noah and his family and all the animals were safe on the ark, for Noah alone had put his faith in the Lord.

Often Carver told stories out of his own experience to impart the essence of his faith. "Mysteries are things we don't understand because we haven't learned to tune in," he said. "And finding true faith in the Creator is solving the greatest mystery of all." Long before, in the home of a wealthy man who knew of Carver's love for music, he had been invited to listen to the radio while his host completed some necessary business elsewhere. "Instead,"

he said, "I sat for an hour in silence. The music was
there, but it was a mystery to me because I did not know
how to tune in."

He urged students to think hard about what they had
to give to others. "I heard one boy offer to share his assets
with another. And the other said, 'No thanks, I'm poor
enough with my own assets.'" When the laughter had
died down—with Carver enjoying his joke as fully as the
audience—he came to the point of his story: money is not
man's most important asset. Peter had no money to give
to the poor cripple, so he offered courage and hope. They,
too, must learn to give what they had—their talent, their
friendship, a cheering word. All the great men of history,
he said, from Jesus to Dr. Washington, had this sainted
sense of giving.

His lessons were always vivid, and sometimes startling.
There were three kinds of ignorance, he said, honest,
stubborn and cussed. The last was the worst, for it was
the curse of not knowing that God loved every one of His
creatures. Once, as a boy, he had been tending some cattle in a pasture when a calf got through the fence and
wandered off after a bull. He had chased it for a while,
then stopped and said, "I will not run another step after
you. You will know whom you're following when suppertime comes." The students waited expectantly, and the
moral was not lost to one of them: in Booker T. Washington's School—as Carver always referred to Tuskegee—
they had an opportunity to fit themselves for lifelong
service and reward; if they failed to apply themselves
and fooled away their time with the "sidewalk boys" in
town, they would know whom they were following when
suppertime came.

It was to his Bible classes that Carver spoke most of

the pungent adages and aphorisms that have been cherished by generations of Tuskegee graduates:

On cigarettes—"If God had intended the human nose to be used for a chimney He would have turned our nostrils up."

On cleanliness—"Your body is the Creator's dwelling place. Surely you would not want a landlord who represents everything good to be seated in an untidy house."

On getting things done—"Back of my workshop there is a little grove of trees. One has been cut down. It makes a good seat. I have made it a rule to go out and sit on it at 4 o'clock every morning and ask the good Lord what I am to do that day. Then I go ahead and do it."

On opportunity—"There is opportunity enough for anyone prepared to do what the world needs done."

On preparation for life—"We must disabuse the people of the notion that there is any short cut to achievement. Life requires thorough preparation. Veneer isn't worth anything."

On the value of the familiar—"Look about you. Take heed of the things that are here. Talk to them. Soon you will hear them talking to you."

On nature—"I love to think of nature as an unlimited broadcasting system through which God speaks to us every hour, if we will only tune Him in."

On death—"One of the things that has helped me as much as any other is not when I am going to die, but how much I can do while I am alive."

Though Roscoe Conkling Simmons, a teacher, called Carver the soul of the faculty, there were some who felt that his view of the Bible was dangerously unorthodox.

Finally they went to the chaplain and complained that Professor Carver's teachings were surely not in strict accord with the Scriptures. The good man pondered this a moment, then asked, "Do many students attend his classes?"

"Yes! and quite a few teachers, as well!" they declared with pious indignation.

"And how long has this been going on?"

"Oh, for years."

"And the class is entirely optional?"

"Yes, but still they persist in attending. It is always crowded."

The clergyman cleared his throat and folded his hands: "Well, then, gentlemen, my advice to you is to say nothing and not in any way trouble this class, for Tuskegee has never had anything approaching such a success, not even when attendance was compulsory!"

Because of their abiding trust in him, students often came to Carver when they were suffering with the rankling hurts of discrimination and prejudice. After America's entry into World War I, many of them had been sent to Howard University in Washington, D.C., for special military training. They were forced to ride north packed into filthy Jim Crow cars—though charged first-class fares—and arrived to be subjected to every slur and indignity which men have ever conjured up to torment their fellow men. They returned deeply troubled, and they said to Carver, "But we went to fight for the United States! And this was the capital of the United States!"

And Carver heard them out, and consoled them as well as he could. And speaking very gently, he said, "No city has a monopoly on ignorance and hatred. There are as many fools in the North as there are in the South, and as many Pharisees in Washington as in Birmingham, Alabama." Then, his arms around their shoulders, he drew them close, as a father might, and said, "You must not let the haters of this world divert you from the path of your own duty. For the time will come when the haters will have been consumed by their own hatred, and the ignorant will have learned the truth. And then, if you are prepared for it, you will walk the earth as free men, the equal of any other man."

Nor would he ever let the white man's bigotry serve as a handy excuse for those who gave less than their best and then summed up their attitude with a bleakly familiar, "Well, what's the use anyway? A Negro can't . . ."

"A Negro *can!*" he always shot back, and once told a group, "Not long ago an important businessman said to me that he wished he knew a man who could find oil. He didn't specify a white man or a black man or a yellow man—just a *man!* And all that man needed was a particular skill that the world was seeking."

To a class of seniors he said, "Perhaps you feel that you can make a useful contribution only in communities where you are wanted. Yet some of you may have to go into areas hostile to you and to your efforts. The invisible 'Not Wanted' sign may be up. But remember all this has happened before. It happened to a man called Jesus when he came to the city of Galilee. Today all men revere Jesus as our Saviour—and remember Galilee only because it was the scene of His ministry."

Carver, of course, was not immune to the spiritual wounds inflicted by bigots, even after his fame was celebrated in every part of the world. When he first came to Tuskegee, he had been cautioned that a Negro in the

South doffed his hat when he talked to a white man, and walked on the street side in the towns so that he could jump down to let a white man pass. He stayed out of the white man's restaurants and hotels and, except for specially-designated sections, out of his theaters and buses. If he drank from the white man's water fountain he might get his teeth smashed, and if he were caught in the white man's neighborhood after dark he might get lynched. And above all, he must never address another Negro as Mister or Mrs. in a white man's presence —that was a title of respect and, as such, reserved exclusively for white use.

The Southern Negro was perpetually on trial. If he did something bad, people said, "Well, what can you expect of a nigger?" If he did something good, they said, "He must have white blood." *

That was in 1896. And four decades later nothing had changed. When Carver traveled, he had to ride in the cramped and antiquated Negro cars, usually right behind the engine and filled with its smoke and soot. Later, when he became famous, he might be sold a drawing room accommodation—it was always done with a wink or a finger to the lips and the understanding that he would be discreet about mentioning it—and of course he dared not venture out of the room, although the journey might last three or four days. He soon learned to draw the curtain whenever the train slowed down or he would almost surely have a rock heaved through the window. He learned, too, to feed himself before going to address a luncheon, else he would sit hungry at the speaker's table, served not so much as a glass of water. Sometimes

* To this day there are otherwise intelligent men who remain rigidly convinced that Carver's genius can be attributed only to a white father.

he would plod the streets of a strange city for hours, searching for a hotel where they would give him a bed to rest his weary bones. Sometimes whites, mere youths, would snarl at him, "Nigger, don't let the sun set on you in this town!"

"No one can know how much courage it took for him to start packing to leave Tuskegee on a trip," said Harry O. Abbott, who accompanied Carver in later years. "Not because he ever thought about his personal safety or welfare, but because he was so sickened by animosity of any kind and he knew he was bound to meet it as soon as he left the protection of the college." Yet as long as he was able to travel, he never refused to go any place where he might cast a light into the darkness.

Once, a United States Senator from Mississippi, remarking on a Carver lecture trip to Southern universities, wondered, "What could that peanut coon from Tuskegee have to say that would be of interest to our boys and girls?"

The tour had been sponsored by the YMCA and Carver's subject was agricultural science. Although he never referred to racial problems, the trip was hailed as "the greatest accomplishment for interracial good will so far achieved in the South," and the result was a first stirring of conscience, a tangible mark of understanding. In one school where the students were forbidden to attend his lecture, they later apologized to Carver in their newspaper: "We wish that race prejudice were a thing of the past in the South," they then wrote. "But the protest raised against Dr. Carver shows that it is still a state to be attained in the future. Some of us are inclined to tuck our heads with shame. But instead of

sitting down and blushing, we should be up and doing
something about it."

Even at the Institute there could be no total defense
against the subtle pricks of bias—and worse. Not long
after the war, the quiet campus was paid a visit by
masked riders of the Ku Klux Klan, and their object was
violence. A Negro veterans' hospital had been planned
for Tuskegee—since Negroes, veterans or otherwise,
could not be admitted to white hospitals in the South—
and the Institute gladly donated the necessary land. All
went well until it was announced that the hospital was
to be staffed by colored doctors and nurses. This infuriated the kleagles and wizards of the Klan—the jobs
constituted a ripe political plum and, besides, it was too
much honor for black people—and they prepared to
ride. The moon was high on the night they assembled
in town and set out for the Institute, their white shrouds
flapping in the wind as they clung to the running boards
of a parade of automobiles, and their numbers were
plain to see as they turned onto the campus road.

But equally plain to see were solid lines of Tuskegee
students, many of them just home from the war for
democracy and standing now ready to defend their
school. The Klan cars slowed while the leaders reeval-
uated the situation—they were not in the habit of fighting for license to spread terror—and then the motorcade
picked up speed again and proceeded right back to the
Old Montgomery Highway. The bloodless battle was
over.

Once a Northern choir came down and, despite the
Tuskegee boys' best efforts to make them feel at home,
behaved throughout an uneasy weekend as though they

ought to be decorated for condescending to appear at a Negro school. When they had finally performed after chapel on Sunday, the small Tuskegee choir took the stage in a spirit of reciprocation. But before they could sing a note, the white boys rose in a body and left the auditorium.

Another time, a group of men walked into Carver's laboratory and, ignoring him altogether, began to inspect the place as though they were in a public museum. Then, still without a word of greeting, nor even so much as removing their hats, one of their number strode up to Carver and declared, "We were driving through and wanted to talk to you. We are from Georgia, but have no prejudice."

To which Carver replied, "Gentlemen, what you do is so loud I can't hear what you say." And he left the room.

Later, an assistant chided him for being curt with his visitors. "They were not sincere," Carver said, "and I am not a curiosity piece."

But with it all, he could never bring himself to a state of real anger, even against the most blatant transgressions. The harshest words anyone ever heard him utter on the subject were, "They can't throw water in my face and make me think it's rain."

He was simply incapable of hatred, no matter what the provocation. Nor did his mind ever think solely in terms of race. He was, as Austin Curtis said, like a parent with a naughty child, grateful for the good, and willing to accept the bad as coming from one who didn't know any better. And, of course, at the bottom, he believed as Booker T. Washington did, that a racist was to be pitied for his blind brutality. And he said, as

Washington so often had, that, "No man can drag me down so low as to make me hate him."

There were, in his day as there are today, those who were militant in the fight for racial equality. Carver was not equipped for this task. "If I used my energy struggling to right every wrong done to me," he once said, "I would have no energy left for my work."

His work was his life, and by not diluting it with wrathful forays against the ignorance of prejudice he was able to make his own unique and most vital contribution to racial amity. He saved the South from poverty—an even more malignant foe of his people than Jim Crow—and thereby earned the gratitude of thousands of whites. And to all the students who passed his way through the long years at Tuskegee, and to a new generation of Negroes who know him from their schoolbooks and the proud memories of their parents, George W. Carver must stand as a magnetic symbol of what a man can do with the hands and the mind that God gave him.

In 1910, the Board of Trustees had voted to establish a Department of Agricultural Research, with Professor Carver in charge. He was relieved of all but a few classes and freed to concentrate on what he called the creative sciences. He would continue to make momentous contributions in an astonishingly broad spectrum of human knowledge—agronomy, nutrition, chemistry, genetics, mycology, plant pathology—but more and more his interests turned to the creation of useful materials from the waste products of agriculture and industry. One day Dr. Frederick D. Patterson, who became Tuskegee's

president in 1935, expressed amazement at Carver's
sometimes intuitive grasp of chemical laws. Carver
shrugged it off. "I use chemistry in exactly the same way
that a housewife uses a cookstove. It is only a tool to get
the job done." He saw all the sciences as tools, means
to an end, and the job he meant to get done was a
lessening of human want.

He believed that the progress of our civilization fell
into three phases. First man *found* the raw materials
that an ever-beneficent nature provided—animals and
plants for food, and wood and stones for shelter. Then he
took those same materials and put some together and
rearranged others, *adapting* them to make metals and
fibers, so they would be more useful to him. Now the
time in man's development had come when it was necessary to *create* entirely new things by making chemical
changes in the old.

"I believe the Creator has put ores and oil on this
earth to give us a breathing spell," he said. "As we
exhaust them, we must be prepared to fall back on our
farms, which is God's true storehouse and can never be
exhausted. For we can learn to synthesize materials for
every human need from the things that grow."

There are those who feel that this sweeping concept,
even yet not fully realized, was Carver's most important
gift to humankind. Never before had anyone advocated
the use of agricultural products for anything but food
and clothing. Never before had anyone envisioned the
familiar farm as a source of raw materials for industry.
In Carver's world of the future, farmers would never
have to worry about markets, nor factory managers
about shortages, and in his lifetime, and because he had
already achieved the impossible in a dozen different

fields, people first came to believe that such a world could come true. In the timeless story of civilization, it took man thousands of years to *find* and utilize nature's bounty, and an industrial revolution to *adapt* it to our modern society. Decades more may pass before we learn to *create* all the things we need to sustain life. But the beginning was made by a colored man named Carver, in a small school in Alabama.

It had all started, of course, with the peanut. But even as he worked to transform the once-useless little goober into 105 tasty dishes and more than 200 totally new products, he was already begun on experiments with the sweet potato which would ultimately beget 118 practical products, ranging from an invaluable wartime wheat to an inexpensive, non-sticky mucilage for the backs of postage stamps. His first step, as always, was to convince the farmers that, with proper soil management, they could raise more sweet potatoes on the same plot of land. In two growing seasons the average yield sprang from 37 to 266 bushels per acre. Then he set about devising ways to utilize the huge harvest—foods, starches and a substitute sorghum syrup. In three years he wrote three bulletins on its care and use.

But sweet potatoes posed a problem: they were perishable. And in showing the farmer how to preserve them longer—by drying on the stove, or even spreading them under a hot sun—Carver laid the groundwork for still another new industry. By the time of World War I, his dehydration studies which Carver called, simply, drying foods—had progressed to the point where he could reduce 100 pounds of sweet potatoes to a powder that fit in a compact carton, kept indefinitely and could be instantly reconstituted by the addition of water.

He had been busy in other ways, too. The war brought its wheatless, meatless and sweetless days, with the shortage of wheat especially acute. Soon Carver had originated a sweet potato flour that saved 200 pounds of wheat flour a day at the Institute alone. With the Allies cut off from German aniline dyes, he perfected an array of 500 substitute vegetable dyes from the roots, stems and fruits of a variety of plants. When a huge dyestuffs firm heard of this, they offered to build and equip a laboratory for Carver, and sent him a blank check, the amount to be filled in by him, if he would accept the job. He declined with gratitude, and along with the check, mailed back the formulas for the 536 dyes he had found to date.

In January 1918, the Army asked him to come to Washington and demonstrate his sweet potato experiments. There was some understandable skepticism on the part of the technical experts—they had already been touted on substitute flour made from barley, rice and chestnuts, and found them sadly lacking—and they waited with hopes held well in check while Carver baked his bread. The result, as he was to say with typical understatement, was that "they were pleased with it and interested in further discussions." Sweet potato flour was soon sent out to Army camps across the country and plans were made for a gigantic dehydration program for overseas shipments.

The latter project never materialized, however, for the war was over before preparations could be completed. With peace, interest in dehydrated food entered a period of hiatus, not to be ended until another world crisis, more than 20 years later. Then, as though George W. Carver had never existed—he was, as a matter of fact, still very much alive—newspapers suddenly began carrying stories about a miraculous new food discovery: dehydration! Edibles of a broad variety, they wrote in wide-eyed prose, could be shipped to our troops in a fraction of their normal bulk, and would never spoil. Why, one company had even succeeded in dehydrating sweet potatoes! Carver remained sublimely—and predictably—undisturbed by the slight. He had often said that there was a 20-year lag, compounded of apathy and cynicism, between laboratory research and the practical application of any radically new idea, and was now only gratified that the development of dehydrated foods, whoever got the credit for it, had proceeded to the point where it proved of genuine benefit to the nation in World War II.

And, of course, that was only the beginning. The dehydrated foods industry is today worth hundreds of millions of dollars, as are frozen foods, a first cousin. And Carver's work goes on still. In 1963 a newly-devised food process involving dehydration and freezing reached consumer markets, and a year later accounted for sales of over $15 million.

All through the years, even when he was deeply engrossed in a major project, Carver somehow found time to respond to the pleas of all who sought his counsel. An average 150 letters were dumped on his desk every morning, and he answered each one in meticulous detail. There were the never-ending problems of the farmers—"You helped me dig a privy in '08 and now it's full. When can you come out and fix it?"—greetings from Tuskegee alumni, invitations to speak, requests for biographical information, and the entreaties of businessmen

willing to pay any price for his collaboration on an
industrial process he had revealed to them in the first
place. Usually his advice cost them only a three-cent
stamp, but a Florida group that had adopted his process
for making lawn furniture out of synthetic marble felt
they could not go on without him. When he declined
a princely sum to join the company, the company came
to him—moving machinery, wood shavings and all, to
Tuskegee, and got the benefit of his regular counsel and
occasional supervision at no cost at all.

In 1930, the Russians extended to him an official
invitation to come to the U.S.S.R. and guide them
through the agricultural phase of their limping first five-
year plan. He declined, politely, as always, and eventually one of his assistants accepted the offer. By that
year, he had written 44 bulletins, ranging from *How to
Raise Pigs for Little Money* to *How to Meet New Economic Conditions in the South*. All were aimed at helping the small farmer help himself—and all, as a matter
of fact, ought to have come out of Tuskegee's Department of Home Economics. But since, in the early years,
no one in Home Economics had the broad knowledge
or the writing skill necessary for the task, Carver had
cheerfully accepted it—he recognized no such precept
as "someone else's responsibility"—and as late as 1942,
when he turned out a wartime best-seller, *Nature's
Garden for Victory and Peace*, he was still writing the
pithy little reports on subjects of vital concern to the
people. Eventually, in an effort to reach a still broader
audience, he started a widely-syndicated newspaper
column, *Professor Carver's Advice*, in which he publicly
replied to the questions most frequently asked him.

Not long ago Austin Curtis said, "The only thing

Carver didn't lick was the boll weevil—and I always suspected that he didn't really want to." But once the weevil had disastrously demonstrated the evils of the one-crop system, and new crops nourished the soil, Carver worked long and hard to improve the South's cotton yield. He had noted that the short stalks produced the fattest bolls, but many were ruined by every heavy rain because, bending to the ground, they were splashed with sand. Patiently he experimented with a cross-breeding process and soon produced the fattest bolls ever on stalks tall enough to hold the plant well up from the sandy soil. Officially recognized, the species was named Carver's Hybrid by the Department of Agriculture.

When other nations began producing cotton in considerable quantity and chemists learned to synthesize rayon and other artificial fibers, the long flush time when every Southern farmer could sell every bale he raised was gone for good. Now Carver began seeking new uses for the cotton that stood moldering in a thousand warehouses. From the stalks stripped by harvest, he had already made rugs and rope and paper, and from short-staple cotton a marvelously light and strong wallboard. Now he came up with a seemingly outlandish idea: the use of cotton in the construction of roads! He began by laying a woven fabric between beds of tar and gravel, a design that proved durable and economic on an experimental section in South Carolina.

But Carver was not finished yet. The woven cloth used only six or seven bales per mile of road, and why go to the expense of weaving it in the first place? So he took just-ginned cotton and fashioned paving blocks from it, using these to bind asphalt together as steel rods are used to bind concrete. Again highway engineers laid a mile of test road—using 40 bales of cotton in the process —and again it met every standard specification, cutting down wear on the asphalt surface in the bargain. Many, many miles of Southern secondary roads were so paved, and otherwise wasted cotton by the thousands of bales were effectively utilized, until finally the development of still-newer processes ended the unexpected boon. But by now flourishing times were again on the horizon for the planters, their markets spurred by the use of cotton in plastics, automobile tires, cardboard boxes, fertilizer and cottonseed oil—uses which, in every case, were pioneered by a Carver concept.

His interest in paints and color washes continued. Eventually he derived a blueing from rotten sweet potatoes which blended well with his clay washes and enabled him to evolve 27 distinct colors. Working with the residue clay, he developed an excellent silver scouring powder and a dust effective against the Colorado beetle, a white potato pest. Then a farmer complained that his rough old weather-boarding cabin drank up the color washes by the bucketful, and that it took as many as five coats before his house was properly covered. This set Carver to pondering the possibility of incorporating an oil base with the clay wash. He found exactly what he was looking for in 30 minutes, or just as long as it took him to walk down to the garage and back to his laboratory. Used crankcase oil, mixed with the wash, made an excellent base and produced a thick, durable paint that still cost nothing but a man's labor. Good ideas, Carver always said, came quickly or not at all, for the best ones were the simplest, and his home-made paint seemed to prove the point: the Tennessee Valley Authority made a grant to Tuskegee for further research, and the paint was eventually to be used at 14 TVA sites as an object lesson in home beautification at nominal cost.

It was another Carver experiment that led to the now-standard use of soybean oil as the base for automobile spray paints. And during World War II, his work with camouflage paint was consolidated with the massive camouflage program then being conducted at Fort Myer, Virginia. Earlier, processing some red clay through various stages of oxidation, he had discovered that rarest of phenomena, a color shade that had disappeared from the world centuries before. It was a royal blue, last used by the Egyptians on the tombs of their dead pharaohs, and lost to man since the end of the Egyptian civilization. And here it was, 70 times bluer than the most intense blue known, in a stretch of clayey soil not far from Montgomery.

When paint manufacturers later learned of the discovery, they deluged Carver by letter and telegram for permission to put it on the market. One even sent a representative to Tuskegee. "Professor," he said with the enthusiasm of ignorance, "we will use your name on it and you will be famous!" The answer, of course, was no —his name would never be used for someone else's profit, nor his own, for that matter, as long as he lived. Nor would he agree to help in any commercial exploitation of his paint, for this could only result in pricing it beyond the reach of the poor farmer. In the end, one company did announce a "new and improved" blue which looked astonishingly like Carver's discovery, but he made no attempt to halt its sale.

He remained available for consultation on problems with the livestock, though some of the younger veterinarians sometimes grumbled, "Well, what does Carver know about cows?" One year, though, they themselves sought his help when six of the dairy herd died mysteriously during a spell of intense heat. Drs. Belvoir and Brown had analyzed the dead animals' stomachs. Dr. Henry had examined the barn and pastures. And still they had no clue to the malady, except that it seemed likely to wipe out the entire herd. Reluctant but desperate, they went to Carver.

"Hm," he said, head tilted back in reflection, "it seems to me we had such a situation some years ago—drought and this same burning heat, day after day."

"We're not concerned about the heat, Professor," said one of the young men impatiently. "The cows . . ."

"Yes, of course." But he seemed to have forgotten they were there. He went scrounging for an old knapsack, edged past them as they stood gaping in astonishment, and disappeared through the door.

Furious, they stalked back to the barn, discharging, en route, some of their tension by reflecting that the heat, whatever else it may have done, certainly seemed to have unbalanced poor old Professor Carver. But in less than an hour Professor Carver appeared in the dairy barn, somewhat wilted from his walk in the pasture, but appearing otherwise of sound mind. He emptied his knapsack at their feet and said, "I think this is your trouble."

They stared at the strange green weeds until one of them found voice. "What is it?" he asked.

"Rattlebox, folks around here call it," was the brisk reply. "The botanical name is *crotalaria*. It grows mostly along the fences and you rarely see it when the fields are green. A cow might nibble a bit and it does no harm,

but when all the grass and most of the other weeds have
been burned out, she'll eat all of this stuff she can find—
it's nice and juicy—and it will poison her."

"Well—well, what can we do?"

"Unless you want some more dead cows, you'd best
take your students out there and dig up as much of it
as you can."

And before they could think to thank him, Carver
had retrieved his knapsack and gone back to Rockefeller Hall to start writing a bulletin on the dangers of
the rattlebox weed. And never again was anyone heard
to say anything that sounded even remotely like, "What
does Carver know about cows?"

Nothing pleased him more than the sobriquet people
had given to him wherever he went, from boyhood on,
and which clung to him through all the years at Tuskegee
—with good reason. The Plant Doctor, they said, could
make nails blossom, and there wasn't a shrub, flower or
weed in all the South that he could not identify by
common and botanical name and precise classification.
Traveling, he would gaze from the train window at the
vegetation flashing by, studying it as a doctor might
examine a patient, and presently he would say, "This
land needs potash," or, "Poor drainage is stifling that
tobacco."

His skill at diagnosing plant ills and prescribing
remedial treatment grew legendary. A blight struck
Alabama's pecans—and Carver found the cause and
cure. A man brought him a branch from a diseased
peach tree—and Carver ground it up, identified San
Jose scale and made up a spray preparation to fight it.
With every changing season he was out prowling the
campus, inspecting the trees, most of which he himself

had planted so long ago. And when he grew too old to climb them, no passing student was immune—nor often surprised—to be handed a saw and asked, "Young man, would you be kind enough to climb up there and cut me that branch, the one with the wilting leaves?" And today the Tuskegee campus is a place of sylvan tranquility, the park of God Carver had visualized, and the practice he began of carefully labeling each tree with both its familiar and botanical name is faithfully continued.

To Carver a weed was only a vegetable growing in the wrong place. Every one had a use, obscured only by men's ignorance. Okra in a cornfield was a nuisance, but cultivated in its own patch made a hearty soup. Farmers ranted at the giant thistle, but it contained definite medicinal properties, as did some 250 other weeds identified by Carver.

Once, walking toward town with young Curtis, he was approached by a forlorn tramp who begged a dime for something to eat. Carver gave him some money and, when the unhappy vagrant had hurried off, said to his assistant, "It's pathetic. Do you realize that in the fence corners between this spot and the nearest place that fellow can buy a meal there is enough nutritious food to sustain him for a week." And pointing to the wild berries flourishing at the roadside, added, "And his diet would be balanced, too!"

Nature, he often pointed out, cast innumerable billions of weed seeds to the autumn winds, and only the sturdiest survived. The result was a plant that had mastered the rules of survival, and usually had more succulence and vitality than the coddled vegetables of the kitchen garden. And he proved his point, introducing dandelions, pepper grass, watercress, chicory and chick-

weed to the Tuskegee dining hall. Of course the precise
ingredients of what came to be called Carver greens
were not revealed to the students until, having been
prepared and seasoned under the professor's direction,
they had turned out to be palatable and, in many cases,
quite delicious.

As was usually the case, Carver's voice seemed to be
heard only by those in immediate earshot—until a time
of crisis. So it was that not until World War II, when
he wrote Bulletin No. 43, *Nature's Garden for Victory
and Peace*, did people in any large numbers discover the
tastiness and economy of the 100 weeds and wild flowers
long recommended by him as nourishing food, including
chicory coffee, a "rhubarb" pie made from curled dock,
and "asparagus tips" of the common pokeweed.

In 1927, he addressed a group in Tulsa, Oklahoma.
His subject, a favorite one, was the Biblical injunction,
"Where there is no vision the people perish." Holding
up a cluster of weeds, he said, "I picked these on Stand
Pipe Hill. Then I went downtown to the drugstore and
bought seven patent medicines, every one of which
contained elements found in these plants. The medicines
had been shipped in from New York City. Why weren't
they shipped from Stand Pipe Hill?"

There seemed to be no limit to his interests and
activity. He found that a certain kind of clay could
effectively replace the expensive gravel heretofore used
on campus paths. From the fruit of the osage orange—
an overgrown shrub used for fence rows—he extracted
a juice that turned the toughest piece of chuck into a
savory and butter-soft steak, the first meat tenderizer.
For diabetics he made a flour that was sweet and easily-
digestible, but contained no sugar. For certain inflam-

mations of the gums, he produced an essence of green persimmon that was always soothing and often a complete cure.

But some of his most far-reaching ideas took decades to materialize. Blessed with vision, he was afflicted by the short-sightedness of the movers and shakers of the time. As early as 1899 he had been urging a comprehensive program of reforestation to prevent erosion and assure an adequate stand of timber for future generations; not until 1932 was such a program officially considered. When the great depression left the agricultural South a veritable tobacco road, it took all the might of the federal government to do what Carver, years before, had predicted needed to be done if the farmers were to be saved. At last a broad start was made on conservation, industrialization and, most important of all, dissemination of practical farming information. All his life Carver battled against waste, and time and again he had warned of the need to develop synthetics. And still it took two world wars before America realized that no nation was rich enough to squander its raw materials without some provision for replenishment.

When his predictions came unerringly true, or when one of his discoveries uplifted a man or a whole people, there were those who extolled him for his far-sightedness, his genius. Carver would have none of it. A man with some particular ability had a responsibility to those less fortunate, he said. "If I were not here, God would find someone else to do His work. That He chose me is no special credit to me."

"Perhaps not," Austin Curtis would later say, "but it is surely a credit to God, and a mark of His infinite wisdom."

IX. The Years of Harvest

TO A SCIENTIST HUMBLY SEEKING THE
GUIDANCE OF GOD, A LIBERATOR TO MEN
OF THE WHITE RACE AS WELL AS THE
BLACK.

—*Citation, Theodore Roosevelt
Medal for Distinguished Service*

In 1938, a speaker introducing Carver to a lecture audience declared, "Socrates once was said to be the world's wisest man because he knew that he knew nothing. Today the man who meets this definition best is Dr. George W. Carver. He, too, knows that he knows nothing, not his parents nor his name nor even the date of his birth. As for the knowledge he gave to the world, he knows only that it came from a power greater than himself."

Carver acknowledged the applause, then, dark eyes glinting mischievously, he said, "I am very disappointed. I always look forward to introductions about me as good opportunities to learn something about myself that I never knew before."

As always, the little gibe warmed his listeners to the subject, which is all it was intended to do. For the fact was that the void in his personal history no longer troubled Carver. He was the personification of a magnificent triumph over the cruel and faceless anonymity

221

spawned by slavery. Perhaps the essential facts of his heritage were lost forever. Perhaps the name he bore was not his own. But the future would compensate him for a shadowy past. His place in history was fixed, and wherever anyone from Tuskegee went, the first question apt to be asked of him was, "Do you know Carver?"

Kings and princes journeyed thousands of miles to see him. He maintained a years-long correspondence with Gandhi, which had begun when he worked out a nourishing vegetable diet for the frail Indian leader, and continued through long letters in which Carver detailed the food values in plants that could easily be grown by the mahatma's starving people. He had the friendship of three presidents—Theodore Roosevelt, Calvin Coolidge and Franklin D. Roosevelt—and when FDR visited the Tuskegee campus in 1940, he asked, as everyone did, for Carver. "You are a great American, Professor," he told the now-stooped and graying old man. "What you have done in your laboratory has made all the nation stronger."

Carver was last in that remarkable succession of Negro leaders, beginning with Frederick Douglass and followed by Washington, whose mission was to *prepare* their people for equality. And like them, he was castigated as an Uncle Tom by a small segment of do-it-now libertarians. He was willing, they said, to suffer the white men's indignities in fair exchange for their support of Tuskegee, and Tuskegee was willing to ignore the aspirations of the handful of specially-gifted Negroes to minister to the pedestrian needs of the mass.

To all of which Carver calmly nodded amen: it was true, as true as the inevitable triumph of his people's cause. But first things first. "I would rather live in a country where every man had a chance to earn a quarter of a loaf of bread," he said, "than in one where a few fattened on whole loaves while the rest of us went hungry." And where would the present generation of Negro leaders have come from, Austin Curtis pointedly asked not long ago, if it hadn't been for the selfless dedication of men like Washington and Carver?

It was in the reticent nature of the man that Carver's leadership was largely a matter of his own inspiriting example. Only among the boys and girls who had sat in his classes, or in that tumbled laboratory—and by now their number was in the thousands—was his benign influence more directly felt, and through them opened out to succeeding circles of young Negroes. And the ripples of light widen still. To the end of his life he kept up a lively correspondence with "his boys" in every part of the world. He rarely forgot a birthday, and in many a modest home across the land the great family treasure is a Christmas greeting from Professor Carver, painstakingly painted in that inimitably gifted hand.

Was a former student in California having difficulty getting into a medical school because of his color? Wrote Carver: "Of course the easiest thing would be to give up —now. But in five years or less you will deeply regret it, and that regret will mark the rest of your life." Later he sent the name of a man who might be helpful.

Did another student need advice on which of two job opportunities to accept? "In assessing the merits of each, list the wages offered you last, and personal benefits next-to-last, and you will not go wrong."

Had an alumnus promised his professional group that Carver would speak to them? Carver would go. Did another need his endorsement to start a country school

in Mississippi? Carver sent it. And no one can say how
many graduates opened an envelope with the Institute
postmark and that familiar angular script to find money,
sent without question or expectation of repayment. The
distinguished roster of Tuskegee alumni now includes
educators, scientists, authors, physicians and United
States Congressmen. And almost without exception each
one cherishes a letter or two from "the professor," a
guidemark at a critical turn in life.

Ralph Bunche, then a fledgling instructor at Howard
University, once came to pay respects to the man he has
called an American benefactor and "the least imposing
celebrity the world has ever known." Carver put aside
his work to talk to the young teacher, and left on him an
indelible impression. "I went away thinking about him
and the respect he was winning from all people, white as
well as black, North as well as South," Bunche has said,
"and I was convinced—for the first time, I think—that
the barriers of race in America were not insuperable."

In 1956, by now a Nobel Peace Prize winner in recognition of his heroic effort in settling the Palestinian war,
Bunche traveled to Simpson College to dedicate a new
science building to Carver's memory. "It is impossible to
calculate the good that has resulted from the social
'chain reaction' which began when Simpson, in 1890,
admitted this unimposing black man," he said—and
might have been speaking of his own historic eminence,
first Negro to be named a division head in the Department of State.

There were other prominent visitors in a steady flow.
The then-Prince of Wales spent hours in Carver's labo-
ratory, fascinated by all he saw. The Crown Prince of
Sweden studied with Carver for three weeks, gleaning

information on the use of agricultural wastes as industrial raw materials. A German official who arrived early one May stayed until after Commencement—and took three graduates back with him to instruct West African colonists in the Carver techniques of crop rotation and land management.

One Sunday Will Rogers came, and after a long afternoon of earnest conversation with Carver, addressed the student body following evening chapel services. He told them how impressed he was with everything he had seen. "But your most valuable possession is that gentleman right there," he said, pointing to Carver. Then, squeezing his voice into a squeaky treble that everyone instantly recognized as an expert imitation of the professor, he added, "He is the only tenor I ever saw who amounted to anything." No one laughed harder than Carver.

Of course his most regular and best-known guest was Henry Ford. They met in 1937, and from their very first exchange the two became fast friends, sharing a restless, unquenchable urge to seek what had never been found, to do what had never been done. They even looked alike, lean and hawk-like, as they sat knee-to-knee in animated conversation, oblivious to the busyness and buzzing around them. Once, when they were being jointly interviewed by the press, Ford said, "Professor Carver can answer all your questions—he thinks exactly as I do." He was enchanted with the watercress sandwiches Carver ordered for their lunch, and thereafter always took a substantial supply away with him.

After their first meeting, they agreed to get together at least once every year thereafter. In the beginning Carver went to Ford's home in Dearborn, Michigan, or to his plantation at Ways, Georgia, where rooms were

always kept in readiness for him. Later, when his health
began failing and he was unable to travel, Ford came
regularly to Tuskegee, and the arrival of his special train
at the siding in Chehaw was the signal for a town-wide
burst of activity. Would Mr. Ford like to see the new
airfield? The most recent addition to the veterans' hospital? He yielded politely, but soon would grow restless,
and say, "May I be taken to Professor Carver now,
please?"

Ford's Tuskegee visits had some far-reaching results,
indeed. Countless whites came to the Institute who never
otherwise would have dreamed of setting foot on a
colored campus. Cordially welcomed and invariably
impressed, they carried away, at the very least, a feeling
of warmth and sympathy for the school's objectives, and
in not a few cases made significant financial contributions. One year, Ford unexpectedly announced to Carver
that he was instituting an on-the-job summer training
program in his plants for Tuskegee students, and not
long afterward, two of his top people were on the
campus recruiting likely candidates. Word that the Ford
Motor Company was hiring colored people contributed
in no small way to the subsequent migration of Southern
Negroes to Detroit.

The very idea of a friendship between the billionaire
apostle of mass production and a $29-a-week agricultural
scientist struck the nation's fancy with its seeming incongruity, and the press made much of it. But the simple
truth was that, apart from worldly wealth—which
hardly mattered, since Ford had a basic contempt for
money and Carver was rich in everything important to
him—the two had much in common: a passion for
productive labor, an unshakable faith in the ability of

man to avail himself of God's gifts and forge a better life. Ford considered Carver a worthy successor to those men of genius—Edison, Firestone, Luther Burbank and John Burroughs—who had been his companions while they lived. "In my opinion," he once said, "Professor Carver has taken Thomas Edison's place as the world's greatest living scientist." Skeptical, perhaps, at the start, he came to be deeply gratified by the discovery that unlike many other men, to whom the power of his money was everything, Carver wanted nothing for himself. In mark of their friendship, Ford built the George W. Carver school for the colored children of Dearborn.

In the great industrialist, Carver had found at last a man with vision and resources enough to make dreams come true. Hard by the Ford laboratories were thousands of acres planted in soybeans. Already Ford engineers were experimenting with many possible substitutions of agricultural products for steel and iron and glass, and in this work Carver zestfully joined in. It would not be long before five pounds of soybeans replaced 25 pounds of metal in American automobiles.

But Carver's most significant work with Ford was in the fabrication of rubber. Fields of goldenrod covered the Georgia plantation, and from this unlikely harvest Carver presently extracted a milky liquid that could be synthesized into a material with distinct rubbery characteristics. It was not as durable as natural rubber, nor would goldenrod, with the vast acreage it required, ever be a practical stock for large-scale production. But an exciting new start had been made in the long search for a synthetic that would fill the rigorous demands of industry at low cost and, once and for all, free the nation from total dependence on far-off sources of supply.

With war clouds darkening, the need was never more urgent. Ford equipped a Dearborn laboratory for Carver, and in nearby Greenfield Village, his classic reconstruction of Colonial America in microcosm, built a magnificent log cabin for the scientist's personal use. But Carver was nearly 80 years old now, and wearying. Moved to tears by his first view of Carver House, outwardly a precise duplication of his mother's old cabin in Diamond Grove, he was fated not to see it again, nor the laboratory with equipment and conveniences such as he had never known. But the work he had begun would be carried forward. Others now had faith that the discovery of an efficient synthetic rubber was within their grasp—and it was. In the year of Carver's death it was already helping to win the war, and today fully a third of all the rubber produced is made by man.

In 1940, when Tuskegee had grown to a campus of 83 imposing buildings, with 2000 fulltime students and a faculty of 200, Professor Carver was still wearing the overcoat he had worn when Grover Cleveland was President. That winter, Harry Abbott, using some travel expense money, bought him a new one which, to no one's great surprise, Carver refused to put on. Abbott then switched from supplication to shock tactics, and finally won the day. "Professor," he said sternly, "this coat cost $125. Surely you wouldn't let all that money go to waste." Carver was aghast—it is unlikely that he had spent as much as $125 for clothing in his entire lifetime —and meekly submitted.

But it was one of his few and final concessions to the flight of the years. He still rose before dawn and worked until well after dark. His equipment remained the simplest—some tin cans, a little one-plate coal stove on which he sometimes also cooked his beloved pigs' feet—and his notes were scrawled on any disreputable piece of paper that came to hand. He still stooped to pick up every scrap on the campus—almost the only time he ever walked on the grass—and still cheerfully submitted to the incredible demands on his time. Rare, indeed, was the week when there was not someone at the Institute seeking his help. In summer Tuskegee was suddenly run through with white students, usually engaged in advanced chemistry research, who got around the Alabama law forbidding them to go to school with colored boys and girls by flocking to Carver's laboratory for "informal" instruction when school was not in session.

One Sunday a delegation of missionaries from some ten African countries called on him. They sat in the second-floor lounge at Dorothy Hall sipping tea and eating watercress sandwiches, and discussed the possible application of Carver's agricultural principles in their respective lands. Could cowpeas be successfully raised by the native people? Soybeans? Carver said that there was no reason why they could not. Then, entirely without preparation, he rattled off an imposing list of grasses indigenous to their separate regions, together with each one's nutritive values and methods of preparation.

Inevitably a growing number of curiosity-seekers and plain busybodies found their way to his quarters. He tried to hold himself aloof from their silly questions and rapacious eyes, but was sometimes forced to abandon the laboratory altogether for the solitude of his bedroom. Then, as often as not, the uninvited visitors would rove about, helping themselves to some piece of his equipment—an earthen vessel that served as a mixing dish, or a milk bottle cut down for use as a beaker. This especially irritated Carver, who always naively believed that the pilferers had some need for the mixing dish or beaker. "But they could have made one with less trouble than it took to steal mine," he would say plaintively, and kept replacing them with other earthen vessels and cut-down milk bottles. And people kept making off with them, deluded—and undoubtedly still deluded—by the prideful notion that they had cleverly come into possession of an authentic artifact from George Washington Carver's original laboratory.

Of course it was an entirely different matter with those who came seeking information, or showed genuine interest in his work. Once a teacher apologetically brought his aging mother to meet the most illustrious member of the faculty. He was already steering her toward the door, profoundly grateful that Carver had politely shaken her hand, when the old lady spied a collection of dried herbs hanging on the laboratory wall. She promptly identified each one as the source of a household remedy, learned years before when she had been a child in slavery. Carver abruptly stopped what he was doing, invited her to sit down, and hours after, having shooed the young teacher off to his classes, the two were still talking earnestly about the curative powers of growing things. Later Carver would say that this woman had known as much about the medicinal values of certain herbs as anyone with whom he had discussed the matter in many years. As for the old lady, she conceded to her son that Dr. Carver did seem to know quite a fair bit about plants, too.

To the end of his days, Carver resisted well-meaning

but inherently narrow-minded attempts to make him fit the pattern of the simple and subservient Negro who, by some wildly improbable freak of fate or, perhaps, by mastering the arts of black magic, had turned out to be a scientist. Mostly he managed this by a gentle ridicule, or by so pointedly exaggerating the witless traits ascribed to him that no one could possibly misunderstand the unspoken rebuke. Once, having misplaced his ticket on a train trip, he was still searching for it when the conductor came to his drawing room. "Oh, don't bother," the man said, recognizing Carver at once, and chuckled meaningfully. "I know how it is with you absent-minded professors. Just send it in when you get back to Tuskegee."

"Yes, thank you," Carver replied, "but you see I don't remember where I'm going." And kept right on looking until he had produced the ticket.

Another time, a businessman seeking to impress Carver with his worldliness and far-flung connections, held forth for half an hour about his dealings and influence in all the great cities. "I don't suppose you ever get far from this place," he finally said. To which Carver answered, "Oh, yes, I've even been to New York. Say, who's the barber there now?"

When a *Time* magazine reporter, after a brief interview, wrote of him as a shabby, toothless old man, Carver pretended to be highly indignant: "Why he just made the whole thing up. If he'd only asked me I would have shown him I'm not toothless at all, for I had my teeth in my pocket the whole time!"

Never did his intense interest in the school or the students slacken. Long acclaimed as the world's foremost agricultural scientist, laden with honors, he still gladly acceded to the baking instructor's periodic requests to give his by-now-famous lecture on the chemistry of bread- and cake-making. And though most of the students who came to hear him were concerned only with the "how" of baking, few left without a heightened appreciation for the "why." He had developed to an uncanny degree the ability to seize hold of an audience's attention, directing his material to a level just barely beyond their easy grasp so that they were compelled to reach for it, and in reaching became totally involved with it. And should he ever sense that he had anything less than every eye and ear, he found a boyish glee in jarring the students back to complete concentration. Thus he once went through the step-by-step procedure for baking bread, then said, "Unfortunately the end result would be unpalatable because I left one thing out. What was it?" Not until the class had exhausted every possibility from sugar to shortening did he tell them: "To light the stove."

He was still refusing all offers of a salary increase, although now the greenest research assistant was earning more than he was. And if there were always those who voiced their astonishment each time he disclaimed any profit from a new discovery, Carver remained equally astounded that they could expect him to claim a private reward for the gift that God had given to him. He kept turning down staggering sums to go to work in private industry, which further grieved the myopics. "But if you had all that money," they said, "you could help your people." To which Carver invariably replied, "If I had all that money I might forget about my people."

The plain truth was that no benefaction of his could ever be so important to the bereft and bewildered souls of the world as the fruits of his genius—new foods from

richer lands, new jobs in new industries, and the great
glowing example of his own noble spirit. And as for
leaving the Institute, he had said all there was for him
to say years before when Thomas Edison had sent his
chief engineer with an invitation for Carver to come to
work in the Edison laboratories in Menlo Park, New
Jersey. His salary was to be a minimum of $100,000. Mr.
Edison himself would shortly come to Tuskegee to talk
over the details.

"There is nothing to talk over," Carver courteously
replied. "I will write my thanks to Mr. Edison, but I
cannot accept."

The emissary was stupefied by this response, and
understandably so: Edison's eminence was worldwide,
his achievements so momentous and his planned projects so ambitious that scientists by the hundreds had
begged for a chance to work with him, and never mind
the salary. And here was an aging teacher in an obscure
little school turning his back on it all, and on $100,000
as well.

Carver must have been perfectly aware of the man's
thoughts as, balked and baffled, he looked around the
meager laboratory and strove to find voice. And Carver
tried to explain: "Dr. Washington brought me here, you
see, and now that he is gone I do not think it would be
right for me to abandon his cause." And then, thinking,
perhaps, that he was not making himself clear, went on,
"I have always worked alone. I would feel out of place
in a large organization such as yours. And there is still
so much to be done here . . ."

And at last Mr. Edison's man understood, as did Mr.
Edison himself when the facts were made known to him.
Expressing his appreciation of Carver's loyalty, he sent

him an autographed photograph, and the two became
fast friends.

Though none of the three Tuskegee presidents who
served during his 46-year tenure could persuade Carver
to accept a salary increase, the last one, Dr. Frederick D.
Patterson, was adamant in his conviction that the vener-
able professor must have an assistant. The sands were
running out. Inevitably there would come the time, and
perhaps soon, when Carver would no longer be able to
maintain his awesome burden of work without some
help. And now, while there was yet opportunity, a
younger man ought to be trained in his methods and
research.

And so all through the early 1930s, a parade of young
hopefuls, one after the other, tapped meekly on the
professor's door, were greeted affably enough—and then
largely ignored. The long years of solitary labor had left
their mark on the old man, and now he tended to forget
that he was no longer alone. And when he did remember,
more often than not the fledgling assistants turned
empty-eyed, hopelessly intimidated by the very idea of
participating in an experiment that no man had ever
before tried.

In September 1935, still another applicant appeared
at Rockefeller Hall. His name was Austin W. Curtis, Jr.,
and he had studied chemistry at Cornell University,
graduating not long before. His father was Director
of Agriculture at West Virginia State College, much of
the land for which his grandfather had donated just
after the Civil War. And as Professor Carver was soon
to learn, young Curtis was an assistant of a totally different stripe.

He was received with at least as much restraint as had
been the lot of his predecessors. Carver shook his hand—
they were still standing in the doorway—and asked,
"When did you arrive?"

"Just now," Curtis eagerly replied. "And I came
directly here."

"Well, perhaps you had better look around the
campus," Carver said. "Get acquainted. Take your time."
And he turned back to his work.

Curtis spent the next six weeks "looking around." Each
morning he reported to the laboratory, and each morning Carver would nod to him—and say scarcely another
word. "It was easy to see why the others left," Curtis
has since said. "You got the feeling that you were about
as important to his work as a used piece of litmus
paper."

But Curtis did not leave. Instead, he decided that if
he could be of no help with Carver's work, he would do
his own. Off-handedly given a bench on the far side
of the laboratory, he began experimenting with the
feasibility of producing a synthetic leather from pumpkin skins. Then he turned to the magnolia grandiflora,
whose seed was rich in an oil that conceivably could
take the place of palm oil in soap, and whose cone
yielded up a pigment-like substance that might make a
suitable paint. And one day Carver came to stand by
his little bench and, after a moment, spoke those magic
words: "What are you doing?"

Curtis told him. Carver asked a few questions more,
then started back to his own worktable. But on the way,
over his shoulder, he said, "Let me know if you need
any help."

Thereafter Curtis did bring his problems to Carver

—but got no easy answers, for that was not the old man's way. Instead, he quizzed his aide narrowly, his piercing questions forcing Curtis into a more rigorous —and rewarding—concentration than the young man had ever thought possible. "My boy, if you are researching, research!" Carver would say. "Do not grope. Now, if your soap is producing too much glycerine you will not find the reason out in the hall or down the street. It is in your formula. How much caustic soda are you using?" And so it went until, all at once, with dazzling clarity, Curtis would see his answer.

When he had been there about two months, an infection of mealy bugs, a greenhouse pest, began attacking many of the campus shrubs, and soon appeared on Carver's cherished amaryllis plants. In a few days, Curtis produced an effective insecticide and after he had dusted the laboratory plants with it, he took a spray gun outdoors and did not return until dark. Whereupon Carver sent him back out to pick up the afternoon mail. The postmaster whistled his amazement. "You might have a chance to stick it out," he said. "You're the first one he's ever let come after his mail."

Curtis laughed wryly: "Thanks, but I'd surely appreciate having a bit more than that to go on."

When he returned, Carver was still working away and scarcely looked up. But Curtis immediately noticed that all his equipment had been moved from the corner over to the main worktable. And so, with not a word spoken, did he learn that the probationary period was over. Not until long afterward did Curtis discover that Carver had weeks before written to his parents to say, "Austin has become what I believed no one could become, an important part of my life and work. He has the intelligence and initiative and creative ability I have sought for years, and I cannot tell you how glad I am that he is with me." Then, in a hasty postscript, he asked them to say nothing of his letter for now.

The new assistant was to be at Carver's side until the end. And Carver would eventually say that the coming of Austin Curtis added years to his life. Surely those years were among his happiest, for young Curtis was almost the son he never had. To have found someone to rely on, someone who could understand his purposes and goals, someone who asked nothing but the opportunity to learn and to help—all this was a bounty such as Carver had never dreamed might be his. Nor could any father have been prouder of a son's achievements. Wherever Carver went, Curtis went—to the Ford plant in Dearborn, to a lecture in Tulsa, to a conference with the Governor of West Virginia—and wherever Curtis went, Carver pushed him to the foreground. He grew equally fond of young Mrs. Curtis, an accomplished artist.

For his part, Curtis became adept at shielding Carver from intrusions, anticipating his needs. Some of the other teachers began calling him Baby Carver and the old professor, delighted, took up the nickname. And between the two, the day long, there was carried on the kind of affectionate raillery that can exist only between men who have become very close indeed. Once, Curtis was to substitute for Carver at a lecture, and read his speech to the professor that afternoon. Carver listened in inscrutable silence, then said, "It's a lovely talk, but you may be the only one who will understand it. You must put the fodder where the cow can reach it."

When his wife returned from a short trip, Curtis

lightly said something to the effect that he would have
to promptly reassert his authority in the household. At
which Carver grinned and said, "I am suspicious of
any man who claims to be boss in his own house. He will
lie about other things, too."

Curtis teased back, and soon became adept at grace-
fully pricking his mentor's grumbling protests against
all efforts directed at his well-being. When Carver complained about the food, the assistant would gently re-
mark, "If I may say so, sir, you are so used to fatback and
peanuts that you don't know what good food tastes like."

On a winter day, when he reproved Carver for walking to the dining hall without a coat, the professor
feigned astonishment and said, "It is amazing, you
know, how I have managed to survive all these years
without you."

"Only by the sheerest luck," Curtis came back.

Carver laughed aloud. "You are turning into a pest,
young man."

But Curtis was to have the last word: "That must be,
sir. Everyone says I am getting more like Professor
Carver every day."

It was Curtis who finally managed to persuade the
press that Carver was considerably more than an un-
tutored mystic who sat back and waited for scientific
revelations from on high. Carver's difficulties with jour-
nalists stemmed from an unpleasantness of long ago,
and because, characteristically, he had washed his hands
of the entire matter and thereafter paid not the slightest attention to what was written about him.

He had been invited to address a religious group in
New York's Marble Collegiate church. Appropriately,
then, his theme was his staunchly-held conviction that

the Creator gave all knowledge to men, and that that
knowledge was intended to be used in the service of
other men. And at one point he said, "No books ever go
into my laboratory. The thing that I am to do and the
way of doing it come to me. The method is revealed at
the moment I am inspired to create something new."

Within days, newspapers from India to England and
in every part of the United States had sensationalized
Carver's extremely subtle meaning in garish headlines.
"Colored Servant Aided By Heaven," they said, and,
"Divine Secrets Revealed to Negro—God His Book of
Knowledge." *The New York Times,* which had not covered the speech, felt constrained to run an editorial
about it which, among other misconceptions, declared,
"It is to be regretted that Dr. Carver should use language that reveals a complete lack of the scientific spirit.
Real chemists do not scorn books and they do not
ascribe their successes, when they have any, to 'inspiration.'"

Carver was deeply wounded by the outcry. It seemed
incredible to him that anyone could so violently misunderstand his words. He had never said that information was in conflict with inspiration, nor that the help
of books and the help of God were mutually exclusive.
He took no books into his laboratory because if the
things he hoped to do were already written down, there
would be no point in his trying to do them. He was a
creative scientist, striving to unlock doors that had never
before been opened, and neither his objectives nor the
means by which he planned to reach them was in any
book. But he had devoted all his life to intensive study,
preparing himself for this work. And whatever he had
achieved was a result of his learning and experience,

without which he could never have aspired to the Lord's essential guidance.

But all these were silent thoughts. Carver never spoke out in his own defense, nor was there anyone to speak for him. And so for years afterward he was regarded in certain sophisticated circles with a kind of skeptical tolerance, a phenomenon of the American legend, the Johnny Appleseed of the peanut fields. They were willing to concede to him certain occult powers, deriving no doubt from his African heritage, but serious scientific grounding and purpose—never.

Nor did Carver ever go out of his way to temper this bizarre judgment. He continued to express himself in the same devastatingly original—and sometimes wildly picturesque—way, using "vision" interchangeably with "idea," referring to his mind as "God's inner workshop" and attributing his discoveries to "divine revelation" in exactly the same sense as a more worldly man would have said, "I had a hunch." And so the newspapers continued to write their tongue-in-cheek stories about Tuskegee's quaint old celebrity, and the doubters were confirmed in their doubts about his professional excellence.

With the arrival of Curtis there was a dramatic change. Where Carver had avoided reporters—leaving them to conjure up their own stories about him, mostly tailored to fit narrow and preconceived notions—his assistant spoke to them in their own language. "When was the last time any of you informed your readers that Professor Carver was a college graduate?" he asked one group. There was a shuffling of feet, but no reply. "Or that he is a collaborator in the Department of Agriculture's Mycology and Plant Disease Survey? Or that he has contributed articles to all of the most respected scientific journals?"

His message was painfully clear, and he kept hammering it home. Another time he recalled for the press that no one found anything to chortle over in the story of Archimedes leaping from his tub, suddenly smitten with his inspiration for the law of the buoyancy of matter. "What is inspiration?" Curtis asked. "Perhaps you gentlemen think it's some cosmic accident. But Professor Carver thinks it is the voice of God, and surely his theory is worthy of as much consideration as yours." Carver's scientific approach was impeccable, he reminded them, his preparation profound, and their disregard for these facts in favor of stereotypes of a strange but beloved visionary was a disservice to both science and religion.

Slowly, sometimes grudgingly, the Carver image projected by the press began to change, sparked by Curtis' persistent appeals to the reporters' essential fairness— and goaded, perhaps, by the cumulation of honors and awards of Carver's later years. And in 1939, when he received the Theodore Roosevelt Medal for distinguished scientific service, *The New York Times* carried another editorial about him, its nature summed up by the concluding sentence: "What other man of our time has done so much for agriculture and the South?"

All through the year that marked the fortieth anniversary of Carver's arrival at Tuskegee, contributions of a dollar or two poured into the Institute. Word was out that a bronze bust was planned to memorialize the occasion—in complete disregard of the professor's acid

objections: "I am not quite ready to be a monument!"—
and plain people everywhere were anxious to have some
small part in it as a mark of their gratitude to the man
who had lifted them from despair. When $2000 had been
raised, the noted sculptor, Steffen Thomas, was commissioned, and on June 2, 1937, the bust was unveiled, a
lofty image of the great soul, eyes gazing confidently
toward a limitless future. Carver himself stood nearby,
bent and graying and ill-at-ease as men spoke of his
contributions to all people. He wore the suit his classmates at Ames had forced on him four decades before,
a jaunty white flower in his lapel, and he tried to make little of it all. But more than one onlooker detected the
tears in his eyes.

It had occurred to Austin Curtis that the moment
might be appropriately commemorated by an exhibit
of Carver's work, sometimes sent on a tour of county
and state fairs, but mostly shut away from public view
in the agriculture building. And so the record of a lifetime's achievement—the thousands of products shaped
from peanuts and sweet potatoes, salvaged from waste
and weeds—were gathered in the new library, with
Curtis himself standing by to explain them to visitors.
And so impressive was the response that President Patterson proposed to the trustees that the display be made
permanent and housed in a separate building, to be
known as the George Washington Carver Museum. If
Carver had any objections, they were swiftly dispelled by
the trustees' choice of a site, the former Institute laundry, a graceful brick building next to Dorothy Hall.

"Well," he said, smiling wryly, "I always felt rather
at home in laundries," and joined enthusiastically in the
organization of the new museum.

In March 1941, Mr. and Mrs. Henry Ford dedicated the building, and a host of fascinated adults and children crowded inside. Here was the Carver mineral collection, here an exhibit of sealed jars containing huge and still-succulent-looking vegetables from the Experiment Station's earliest harvests. There were samples of his paints, including the incomparable Egyptian blue, his dyes and stains and wallboard, and in a partitioned area, nearly 100 of his paintings and sketches, and a broad selection of his lacework and crocheting.* There was also an office and laboratory for Carver's use, so that the Museum became not only a record of the past, but a source of continuing creativity.

Meanwhile laurels in accelerating number and sweeping scope marked the growing esteem in which he was held around the world. Long before, he had been one of the few Americans elected to a Fellowship in Great Britain's most exalted scientific body, the Royal Society of Arts, and some years later won the Springarn Medal for distinguished research in agricultural chemistry. In 1928, Simpson, his beloved alma mater, conferred on him an honorary doctorate in science, President John L. Hillman calling him the college's most esteemed son, and rejoicing that, "We did not fail him when he came knocking for admission." In 1941 the University of Rochester sent a delegation to Tuskegee to grant him a second honorary degree. A Carver study in brown and silver by artist Arthur Leroy Bainsfather won a prize for the loveliest painting of a Southern subject, the jury announcing that its spiritual beauty transcended the physical aspects. And Carver's own exquisite portrait called

* A disastrous fire at the Museum in 1947 destroyed many of these irreplaceable artifacts, including most of the paintings.

Four Peaches was chosen for exhibit in the famed Luxembourg Gallery in Paris. Some 18 schools across the country had now been named for him, which gave the old professor—who had never lost his conviction that a school was a hallowed place—more joy than all his other plaudits and kudos.

There were some curious contrasts. The Governor of Alabama proclaimed a Peanut Week and Carver was escorted to the parade line by a platoon of motorcycle policemen. But a list of Missouri's ten greatest sons, published not long after his death, did not include his name. And there are those who believe that the only reason he was never awarded a Nobel prize was because his skin was black.

Early in 1940, Carver indicated his desire to bequeath his savings—which, thanks to his fantastic frugality, amounted to some $33,000—to the Institute, not after his death, but now, when he might have a hand in how it was used. He responded favorably to a suggestion that the George Washington Carver Foundation be established. On February 10, it was signed into being, its purpose to provide facilities and a measure of support for young Negroes engaged in advanced scientific research. Of course $33,000 would not provide all that was needed, but after an intensive fund-raising campaign, spurred by such diverse personalities as Edward G. Robinson, the movie actor, and Henry Ford, sufficient money was accumulated to begin work in the Carver Museum— and very much in the Carver image: among the earliest projects was a contract with a sugar refining company for research in the uses of various fibers.

At Carver's death, all the rest of his estate went to the Foundation, making his total contribution $60,000. Funds continued to come in from those who shared his dream, and from commercial research projects, and eventually a $2 million building was erected to house the facilities for advanced study in botany, creative chemistry, mycology, plant genetics and agronomy. And for hundreds of gifted young men and women who never knew Carver, but without him might well have seen their talents stultified, and perhaps killed altogether, the Foundation was the old professor's most meaningful contribution.

Now under the direction of Dr. Clarence T. Mason, it carries on in precisely the circle of research by which Carver enriched the South with new crops, then invented uses for them. Some students are experimenting with certain teas never before grown in this country, others are studying strontium absorption by food plants. And perhaps today, perhaps tomorrow, there will walk into the George Washington Carver Foundation a young man or woman with the same dazzling genius, the same single-minded determination to push beyond the frontiers of existing knowledge as possessed by that threadbare teacher of agriculture who came down to Tuskegee from the West in '96, and in laboratories that George Carver made possible a new start will have been made toward reshaping our world.

For as long as he lived, Carver remained concerned with the welfare of the students who still flocked to his Bible classes and still sought his private counsel at every hour of the day. Returning from a trip to Tulsa, he told them, "As I looked at the giddy young people jazzing around on the street, my thought was, 'How much can the world depend on you?'" He studied his own cherished boys and girls now, and said, "Do not let the world down, and you will never let yourselves down."

For their part, the students revered him, and worried constantly about his health. When Austin Curtis was traveling extensively on the business of the newly-formed Foundation, they took to walking past his laboratory door and peeking in to make certain that all was well. This seemed to distract Carver, who complained that if he had wanted someone interrupting him all day he would have married. Whereupon the students offered him an alternative: to have a small glass window built into the heavy laboratory door so they could "make rounds" without troubling him in the slightest. Carver fussed and fumed, but in the end the youngsters had their way and the glass pane was installed.

It was clear that Carver was weakening. In 1937 he had been hospitalized for pernicious anemia, and those who knew him best felt that only because his interest had been captivated, first by the Museum, and then the Foundation, was he restored to a measure of his former vigor. When he was released, new quarters were assigned to him in Dorothy Hall, the guest house, so he could be close to the Museum. When Henry Ford visited him there and saw him struggling up the exhausting flight of stairs, he had a private elevator installed to open directly into Carver's rooms.

Still he sometimes breathed with great difficulty, and his weakening heart hammered alarmingly in its effort to pump life through that frail and toilworn body. The very smell of food sickened him, and now his meals, such as they were, were brought to his quarters on a tray. But his pixy sense of humor remained indomitable. A new dietician bustled in one evening, whipped out her pad and, in best businesslike manner, said, "And what would we like for dinner tonight?"

"I have no idea what you would like, young woman," the professor replied, "but you may put that pad away. I assure you that you can easily memorize all I would like."

The cooking teacher, Mrs. Juanita Jones, could sometimes tempt him with favorite dishes, and by paying meticulous attention to the overall appearance of his tray—a fresh flower, appealing colors—which Carver insisted enhanced the palatability of any food. Once, discouraged because he had eaten practically no dinner, she said she would fix anything he wanted for breakfast if he promised to finish it. He asked for pancakes—"the little ones, and in quality, please!"

Mrs. Jones rose at dawn next day and, before her first class, brought him three half-dollar sized pancakes, done precisely the way he liked them. She was delighted when he downed them without a murmur—and thrilled when he slyly said, "I would rate those good in quality, but poor in quantity." And she rushed off to make some more.

Toward the end of 1942, when he fell ill again, he refused to see a doctor. "There is nothing to be done," he said matter-of-factly, "and I am not going to let them press a cold stethoscope against my chest."

But again Mrs. Jones won out. "Surely you wouldn't offend Mr. Henry Ford. He has sent his own specialist all the way from Detroit," she lied with a perfectly straight face.

"He did?" said the old man, pleased. "Well, all right."

Mrs. Jones promptly slipped into the next room and telephoned the Veterans' Hospital, and a young doctor,

properly briefed—and advised to pre-warm his stethoscope—was allowed into the sickroom.

But as was usually the case, Carver was right: there
was nothing to be done. He was past eighty years old,
and the body that housed that great soul and spirit was
wearing out. A few days after Christmas he sent for Dr.
Patterson and handed him a sheaf of United States savings bonds. "I want these to go to the Foundation," he
said, "and I want the world to understand clearly that I
bought them because a man's color has nothing to do
with the love he feels for his country."

Systematic to the last, Professor Carver was putting
things in order.

X. A Time to Die

IT IS SIGNIFICANT THAT BECAUSE HIS
BIRTHDAY IS UNKNOWN, WE HONOR HIS
DEATH-DAY. THIS IS THE DAY ALL SAINTS
ARE HONORED, THIS DAY WHEN THEY ARE
BORN INTO THE FULL SIGHT OF GOD.

—*Clare Boothe Luce*

H E NEVER spoke of death. It was such a familiar part of life, the companion of every autumn. But in spring there came the time of rebirth, and so life went unwaveringly on.

He remained alert to the very end, reading the frayed leather Bible Mariah Watkins had given him on that long-ago Christmas morning, and asking all who came to see him for the latest campus news. At 5 P.M. on January 5, 1943, Mrs. Jones brought his dinner, but he took nothing except a few sips of milk. She hadn't even the heart to chide him as he lay back on his pillows, exhausted.

"I think I'll sleep now," he whispered to her, his eyes already closed, and she collected the dinner things and tiptoed out.

And sometime in the next two hours the valiant heart just stopped beating, and without struggle or pain his imperishable soul slipped from a spent body.

The sad news was announced that evening, first to

the students, and then to the world. Stunned and griev-
ing, the young people and the teachers and the townfolk gathered in sad little clusters, standing together
but saying nothing. It seemed inconceivable that he
was gone, for he had been as much a part of Tuskegee
as the very land it was built on.

Reuben A. Mundy of the Agricultural Department
remembers hurrying home to tell his wife. They were
going to have a child shortly and had hoped that Professor Carver would give it his blessing. When Mundy
reached his front gate, he knew at once that his wife
had already heard. She was standing alone by the great
camellia tree that Carver had years before planted for
them as a spindly seedling, and she was weeping.

Juanita Jones walked slowly home, conscious only of
holding the flower that had been on the professor's dinner tray. And in the laboratory, Austin Curtis gazed
numbly at the amaryllis plants that had been Carver's
last work—he had been cross-breeding them to multiply
their gay red stripes—and now and then gently touched
one.

Soon the messages from the great men of the world
began to pour in. President Franklin D. Roosevelt wrote
that he counted it among his great privileges to have
known Carver. Vice-President Wallace, remembering
back nearly half a century when the tall teacher at Iowa
State had held his small boy's hand and revealed to him
the secrets of the plants and flowers, said, "The United
States has lost one of its finest Christian gentlemen."

And out where the roads ended, in the hills and
swamps, the men and women who worked the land and
could find no words for their sorrow, wept in silence.

Before long a bill was introduced to the 79th Con-

gress by Senator Harry S. Truman of Missouri, providing
for the establishment of the George Washington Carver
National Monument on the site of the original Moses
Carver farm near Diamond Grove. It was to be accepted
into the national parks system and house "records and
relics pertaining to George Washington Carver, and
other articles of national and patriotic interest."

Expressing the State Department's endorsement of
this proposal, Assistant Secretary Adolf A. Berle, Jr.,
wrote to the Committee on the Public Lands: "Dr. Carver's career has done us honor; and it is fitting that we
should delight to honor him. But more than that, his
life of quiet devotion to his fellow man is a bright spot
in these dark days of hatred. A national monument is
none too strong a reminder of all he stands for."

The bill passed without a dissenting vote.

When the monument was dedicated, the New York
Herald-Tribune wrote: Dr. Carver was, as everyone
knows, a Negro. But he triumphed over every obstacle.
Perhaps there is no one in this century whose example
has done more to promote a better understanding between the races. Such greatness partakes of the eternal.
Dr. Carver did more than find hidden merits in the
peanut and sweet potato. He helped to enlarge the American spirit."

He had died without known relatives, yet through all
the days that he lay in the chapel, serene and at peace, a
perfect white camellia in his lapel, the long lines of people continued to wind past the bier. They had come by
car and bus and on foot for this final farewell, from the
nearby countryside and from the far reaches of the great
land. And Chaplain H.V. Richardson welcomed them,

and said of the man who had been a friend to each of them, "He worshipped God by drawing out of the things that grow goodnesses that served the needs of mankind."

On the fourth day they carried him up to the hill where Dr. Washington had rested these 27 years and more, and they lowered his mortal remains into the earth. And his epitaph was, "He could have added fortune to fame, but caring for neither, he found happiness and honor in being helpful to the world."

Then the sad lines of people started down the hill, the memory of him still so strong that a world without him seemed impossible to imagine. And there was a great stillness on the land, and the night turned cold and winter-dark. But in the sheltered places buds had begun swelling, and anyone who sought comfort that night could find it, for another spring was coming.

Bibliography

Bontemps, Arna. *The Story of George Washington Carver.* Grosset & Dunlap, New York, 1954.

Borth, Christy. *Pioneers of Plenty: The Story of Chemurgy.* Bobbs, Merrill, New York, 1939.

Bullock, Ralph W. *In Spite of Handicaps.* Association Press, New York, 1927.

Campbell, Thomas M. *The Movable School Goes to the Negro Farmer.* Tuskegee Institute Press, 1936.

Clark, Glenn. *The Man Who Talks with the Flowers.* Macalester Park Publishing Company, St. Paul, 1939.

Graham, Shirley and Lipscomb, G.D. *Dr. George Washington Carver Scientist.* Julian Messner, Inc., New York, 1944.

Holt, Rackam. *George Washington Carver: An American Biography.* Doubleday and Co., New York, 1943.

Imes, G. Lake. *I Knew Carver.* Printed by J. Horace McFarland Co., Harrisburg, Pennsylvania, 1943.

Jenness, Mary. *The Man Who Asked God Questions—George Washington Carver.* Frontier Books No. 1, New York, 1946.

Johnson, F. Roy. *The Peanut Story.* Johnson Publishing Co., Murfreesboro, North Carolina, 1964.

Mathews, Basil. *Booker T. Washington.* Harvard University Press, Cambridge, Massachusetts, 1948.

Means, Florence Crannell. *Carver's George.* Houghton Mifflin Co., Boston, 1952.

Merritt, Raleigh. *From Captivity to Fame.* Meador Publishing Co., Boston, 1938.

Richardson, Ben. *Great American Negroes.* Thomas Y. Crowell Co., New York, 1945.

Smith, Alvin D. *George Washington Carver: Man of God.* Exposition Press, New York, 1954.

Washington, Booker T. *Up From Slavery.* Doubleday, Page and Co., New York, 1900.

255

Washington, Booker T. *Tuskegee and Its People*. D. Appleton
and Co., New York, 1905.

———. *My Larger Education*. Doubleday, Page and Co., New
York, 1911.

Selected Articles, Pamphlets and Public Addresses:

American Men of Science. George Washington Carver. Page 230.
Science Press, New York, 1938.

Bulletins, The Experiment Station, Tuskegee Normal and Industrial Institute, Nos. 1 through 44, 1898–1943.

Bunche, Ralph. The World Significance of the Carver Story. An
address at Simpson College, Iowa. October 6, 1956.

Campus Digest, The (Tuskegee Institute). Professor Carver's
Bible Class. March 2, 1927.

Carver, George Washington. A six-page handwritten autobio-
graphical sketch, probably written around 1898.

Childers, James Saxon. The Boy Who Was Traded for a Horse.
The Reader's Digest, Page 5. February, 1937.

Current Biography. George Washington Carver. Page 16. November, 1940.

House of Representatives. Hearings before the Committee on
Ways and Means. January 21, 1921.

Lorch, Fred W. George Washington Carver's Iowa Education.
The Iowan, Fall, 1964.

Luce, Clare Boothe. The Saintly Scientist. An address. January 5,
1947.

Newsweek. Dr. Carver, Miracle Worker. Page 84. April 5, 1943.

Pammel, L.H. A letter about Carver's life from his former teacher
at Iowa State College, 1928.

Reader's Digest. No Greener Pastures. Page 71. December, 1942.